To Cathy, Brian, Troy, and Gail, my partners and co-navigators in LogoLounge; to Susan, Luke, and Mason of Gardner Design, for keeping the ship leveled out when I bury myself in these books; thanks especially to Elisabeth of Gardner Design for her tireless diligence in assembling the work of our exceptional members for publication; to Kristin at Rockport for keeping these books a joy to produce; and mostly to Andrea and Molly, the loves of my life.

–Bill Gardner

To Alex, Andrew, and Sam, my sons and mentors—thank you.

–Catharine Fishel

contents

introduction

LogoLounge.com and the LogoLounge book series have been so overwhelmingly embraced by the design community that at times I almost feel a bit embarrassed. Members of the site and readers of the books have asked time and again about their success. The marriage of the site and its books are complex when you start to consider all they offer and the diverse ways they are used. But I have narrowed the answer down to one word: context.

There's another word that is nearly as critical as context—its near twin, content. Since the site's inception at the end of 2001, LogoLounge.com members have submitted more than 37,000 logos as of early 2006. Our thousands of members represent every top-tier identity firm in the world and nearly every nation on Earth. They also represent the genius of small studios that know how to help their clients thrive as top-tier competitors.

Every day, more logos are uploaded to LogoLounge.com, and as amazing and stimulating as these thousands of logos are, they would be perilously close to useless without context. Imagine your desk heaped with 37,000 individual logos, each on a separate slip of paper and in no particular order. It would be of modest value to anyone. Looking for logos of globes, or birds, or leaves, or for a coffee house, or the letter "E"? You could just start digging and, depending on your stamina, you might eventually find something inspirational. Or, if you really had months to invest, you could start to organize the heap.

This absurd situation is pretty close to what happens when you try to find something specific in the mass of books on your shelves, each with its contents randomly organized. Spontaneity is good, but not when you're under the gun and need very specific reference. This is why the book you're holding is filled with 2,000 logos, meticulously organized to allow you to intuitively find inspiration wherever you look and exactly where you expect it.

To add to the book's value, its 2,000 logos are further organized on a companion website at www.logolounge.com/book3. When you log onto this site, you will be able to use the same search tools that LogoLounge.com members use when searching the nearly 38,000 logos on the site. You can search the contents the way you want to—by keyword, client, industry, designer, style, or date, and even link to a designer's website or email.

This book delivers another sort of rich context, too: dozens of in-depth stories behind the birth of some of the most influential identity projects of our time. Travel through the back-story and the boardroom as designers weave through challenging obstacles to create visual identities for the likes of Sprint, the Beijing Olympics, Australia, AOL, Unilever, Bank of New York, and Target's private label Archer Farms, to name a few.

Why go to all this trouble? Because we think your time is important. The LogoLounge book series and website put inspiration at your fingertips in an instant so that you can spend more time designing and less time playing librarian for the creative universe.

—Bill Gardner

jurors

Emanuela Frigerio
C&G Partner, New York, NY

The Dog House logo, by DDB Dallas
"My favorite design is the The Dog House pet groom-
ing logo. I love its simplicity. It is clear, memorable, and
timeless—all the attributes a successful logo should
have. Though it unmistakably communicates that this
is a pet grooming service, it also suggests a business
that is caring and professional. The form is pleasing,
and the one-color black solution, while basic, is perfect.
I have to admit, it even made me smile, which is a rare
quality for a logo, indeed."

Born and educated in the *fulcro* of Italian fashion and industrial design, Emanuela Frigerio has worked in London, Milan, Tokyo, and New York. Clients have included IBM, Knoll, the Museum of Modern Art, the Library of Congress, the U.S. General Services Administration, the Rockefeller Foundation, Harry N. Abrams, Crane & Co., and the McNay Art Museum.

A 15-year principal at Chermayeff & Geismar, Inc., she designed a 352-page monograph called *designing* that covers 45 years of the firm's work. She is currently a principal at C&G Partners together with Steff Geissbuhler, Keith Helmetag, and Jonathan Alger.

Connie Birdsall
Lippincott Mercer, New York, NY

Central Christian Church logo, by Mindspace
"I chose this logo because it engaged me and pulled
me into the design on a couple of levels—initially, the
sheer restraint and striking elegance of the forms, and
then the beautiful discovery of the characters holding
hands when you take that second look. Such a won-
derfully simple design solution resonates so strongly on
many levels: The cross symbolizes Christianity, the peo-
ple forms represent the church, and the simple use of
color communicates the conflict resolution aspect. You
don't even need the words. Then, you just can't get it
out of your mind. It's sticky and memorable, more signs
of a really effective logo design. When a designer gets
the execution of the elements just right from a formal
graphic perspective and tells a compelling story, it's a
real accomplishment. The overall impression of the logo
projects a real sense of humanity that leaves me with a
positive, hopeful, and uplifted feeling."

Connie Birdsall, creative director and senior partner at Lippincott Mercer, has spent 20 years creating global corporate and brand identity programs, marketing communications systems, information design, launch and implementation programs, and brand management tools. She has led the creative development of branding programs in Asia, Europe, Latin America, and the United States for clients such as Samsung, Citigroup, IBM, Continental Airlines, and, most recently, the Bank of New York and SK Group in Korea. A member of the National Board of Directors of the American Institute of Graphic Arts (AIGA), Birdsall holds a BFA from the Kansas City Art Institute and an MFA from Cranbrook Academy of Art.

Graham Purnell
Cato Purnell Partners, Melbourne, Australia

Doglogic logo by Elephandt in the Room

"My choice is Doglogic. It made me laugh. The designer obviously understood the core of what had to be communicated and how to do it with style, intelligence, and humor. A great idea, well executed."

Graham Purnell is partner with Ken Cato in Cato Purnell Partners. Under his creative direction, the firm has acquired new clients in a range of industries both in Australia and overseas. After earning a master of art degree from the Royal College of Arts in London in 1984, Purnell worked as senior designer at Minale Tattersfield. He subsequently worked in Singapore with Batey Advertising as design director.

Purnell's work has appeared in many international design publications, including *D&AD, Graphic,* and *Design Downunder.* His work for Energex, Coles Farmland, Kraft, Nestlé Nescafé, Primelife, Royal Guidedogs Association, and Suncorp Metway, and many other clients has earned a number of awards for Cato Purnell Partners.

Miles Newlyn
London, England

Kathy Taylor/Acupuncture & Chinese Herbalist logo, by Kahn Design

"I selected Kathy Taylor/Acupuncture & Chinese Herbalist as my favorite. I liked it because it drew me in and made me feel comfortable with alternative medicine. It could be read a number of ways—I like that—but one that appealed was that of knowledge passed from generation to generation. Hands are notoriously difficult to use in logo design, whilst offering great symbolism. This logo used the element of a hand in a way that circumvented the inherent awkwardness, resolving in a beautifully contained shape. A delicate but potent touch."

Miles Newlyn is a renowned typographer, thinker, and designer. He has worked for the world's top branding agencies to create identities for some of the world's leading businesses. Newlyn applies his talents to custom type design as well as logo design and is known for pushing the boundaries of the corporate sector. He has designed many famous logos, including marks for Honda and Unilever, and is also known for helping clients break out of twentieth-century communications strategies and talk today's language of hyperindividualism. Cult designer David Carson describes him as a "type designer extraordinaire," but Newlyn says he simply "designs for people, not markets."

Thomas Vasquez
Brooklyn, NY

MetaCosmetic logo, by GRAF d'SIGN
Creative Boutique

"Extremely attractive, the MetaCosmetic logo is curvaceous but not overweight, slender without being too thin. It exudes sexuality, has a timeless personal style, expresses originality of thought, reproduces well, is a bit mysterious, and has a sense of humor. But above all, it is smart—and because of that, beautiful. The main problem: It is only a logo."

Since starting his career in the early 1990s in Dallas, Texas, Thomas Vasquez has shaped the way ideas and voices are expressed for some of the world's best-known brands. He has worked with Ogilvy & Mather's Brand Integration Group, creating solutions for IBM, Miller Brewing Co., and Maxwell House, after which he moved to the production company Cyclops. There he created print design and advertising for Levi's, Jockey International, and Universal Music Group, as well as title design work for RCA, ABC, and NBC. He also led the team responsible for rebranding one of the world's most recognizable icons, Elvis Presley.

After leaving Cyclops in 2004, Vasquez began consulting as a freelance design director to advertising agencies: Ogilvy & Mather, BBDO, J. Walter Thompson, DDB, and Berlin-Cameron. He also freelances as an art director for the Sunday edition of the *New York Times.* Most recently, he was chosen by Deutsche Bank to participate in a three-month public art exhibition celebrating the International Book Fair in Frankfurt, Germany. Vasquez has lectured on the subject of branding and identity design, and his work has been published in just about every national and international book and periodical on graphic design and advertising.

Robert Matza
Landor Associates, New York, NY

Eléctrica Bahia, by Oficina de Diseño y Marketing

"Simple, clean, well-balanced positive and negative space, and timeless: all ingredients for a successful mark. The electrical plug is clear and an appropriate message for this company. I was surprised and pleased, at second glance, to discover the hidden letter E. I appreciate the honesty and lack of frivolous decorative noise."

As creative director of Landor Associates New York, Robert Matza brings more than 17 years of experience to his corporate identity clients. In addition to working closely with his design team, Matza collaborates with all other disciplines within the office, including naming, strategy, and new business marketing. Since joining Landor in 1997, he has directed identity programs for Morgan Stanley, GE, PepsiCo, Tenaris, Computer Associates, New York Stock Exchange, Vanguard Group, Lenovo, Cleveland Clinic, Verizon, and Nielsen Media Research. More recently, he built programs for Bristol-Myers Squibb, Citigroup, and IBM. Matza also serves as creative director of Klamath Communications,

a specialized group that delivers a full spectrum of integrated communications to select Landor clients.

Prior to joining Landor, Matza spent 4 years at Chermayeff & Geismar, where he worked with clients such as Sony Entertainment, Telemundo, Mobil Corporation, and Simon & Schuster. He has lived and worked in Madrid, Spain, and through client relationships in South America and Europe he has developed extensive international experience. He holds a BFA in Graphic Design from the Rhode Island School of Design and volunteers his time and services for many nonprofit organizations.

Kit Paul
Brandient, Bucharest, Romania

Canadian Museum for Human Rights — Winnipeg,
for Ralph Appelbaum Associates, by Polemic Design
"This is a piece of work I really admire. The designer
achieved a groundbreaking effect by understated,
almost humble means, cleverly embedding right into the
logo the value this brand stands for: the belief that
human rights always come first. Also, I've never seen
such a dramatic representation of the truth in Victor
Papanek's statement that 'design is the conscious effort
to impose a meaningful order' — my favorite definition of
design seen from quite a literal, unexpected angle."

Cristian "Kit" Paul is a founding partner and creative director of Brandient, the Romanian brand strategy and design consultancy. Before setting up the consultancy with his partners, he cut his teeth on many advertising campaigns and won coveted national and international nominations and prizes while working as an art director and creative director with the advertising agencies Graffiti/BBDO, Tempo, and D'Arcy DMB&B in Bucharest. He also worked as a freelance graphic designer in Romania and Singapore. Presently, Paul is deeply rooted in corporate identity while publicly advocating the role of design.

HUMAN RIGHTS CANADIAN MUSEUM FOR

Sharon Werner
Werner Design Werks, Minneapolis, MN

Mjólka logo, by Ó!
"Smart, simple, memorable, cute. What more could
you ask?"

Sharon Werner founded the Minneapolis-based design firm Werner Design Werks, Inc., in 1991. The small studio specializes in combining strong visual language with sound design solutions to create work that affects not only commerce but culture. The office has worked with Target Corporation, Mohawk Paper, Chronicle Books, Mrs. Meyer's Clean Day, Blu Dot Design and Manufacturing, Nick at Nite, VH1 Networks, Levi's, Minnesota Public Radio, and Moët Hennessy.

Werner's office has garnered national and international awards and honors, and was named the Target Corporation's Vendor of the Year in 2002. WDW's work is included in *100 World's Best Posters* and is part of the permanent collection of the Library of Congress, the Rumpus Room of Ernest and Viola Werner, Musée de la Poste, Victoria and Albert Museum, Musée des Arts Décoratifs, and the Cooper Hewitt Museum.

portraits

Design Firm	Desgrippes Gobé
Client	America Online
Project	Corporate Identity Redesign

In 2003, America Online was becoming increasingly irrelevant to consumers, and in more than a few instances it was referenced as "training wheels for the Internet," especially as consumers were moving quickly from dial-up to broadband access.

"In truth, AOL was one of the first proponents of high-speed connections. But consumers did not relate that to AOL," notes Marc Gobé, principal and chief creative officer for Desgrippes Gobé, New York City, the design firm that undertook the rebranding for the online giant. "The company needed a new image and message in order to change perceptions."

> It was really important to show AOL's commitment to society.

In its early days, America Online worked hard to dispel the fears many people had about using the Internet—indeed, about using computers at all. Its friendly, helpful image (like that of a cheerful primary school teacher) resonated with users. As the company moved into broadband and wireless and added high-tech services, however, it had to confront newcomers such as MSN and Yahoo.

America Online did have one powerful attribute that the others did not: a tremendous emotional connection with customers.

"Historically, AOL is like a friend with a comforting nature. It gets people on the Internet in an easy way. We needed to move from that into a position of being a savvy, trusted partner. AOL offers products and services that are innovative and smart, but it also offers security and protection for families. It was really important to show their commitment to society," Gobé explains.

Desgrippes Gobé worked with the AOL brand strategy team to ensure that the new visual identity was aligned with a new positioning that focuses on fighting for the consumer. This focus is now echoed in the tagline, "Want a better Internet?"

Regaining a leadership position while maintaining that emotional relationship—a relationship critical to customer loyalty—would be a tricky proposition. Gobé says the new positioning had to demonstrate that the service was on the customer's side, looking out for him or her and truly caring about the online experience.

(Above left) Desgrippes Gobé gave AOL's logo an interesting new slant—literally. When the old logo was turned just slightly, it became an arrow pointing AOL users to the future.

(Above right) AOL's logo was familiar to anyone on the Internet—too familiar, in fact. It had become such an integral feature of the cyberspace skyscape that it was almost invisible.

AOL's new three-dimensional logo is brought to life in an innovative CD package that reinforces the shape whenever the customer comes into contact with it. The case was also used as a 3-D graphic in retail displays (right).

15

Changing the triangle into an arrow transformed the logo from a marker to a message.

Degrippes Gobé also designed an AOL experiential store in New York City that turned the brand into a sensory experience. It contains a sound studio where people can listen to music and an electronic bar with computers for sending email or photos taken in the store. Some of the photos were used to build a mosaic of faces. "In sharing your face, you were showing you were part of a much larger community. A huge part of the Internet is a sense of community," explains DGA principal Marc Gobé.

We float in space and have the freedom to reach new dimensions. This logo also lives in space.

There is some danger in changing a familiar logo, he notes. On the other hand, when a logo becomes too familiar, it loses its meaning and becomes, essentially, invisible.

The original AOL triangle mark had value as a recognizable shape, but it had faded into the background of cyberspace. Gobé wanted to transform it into something new: with a slight tilt, the triangle could be turned into an arrow pointing forward into the future.

"We did not have to stick with the triangle, but the shape had such awareness among the company's 20-million-plus users. Current and past AOL members consistently recalled two elements of the current logo as key to what AOL stands for—the color blue and the triangle. Changing it into an arrow transformed the logo from a marker to a message," the designer says.

The arrow announced the company's commitment to guiding users to new experiences and continually providing new features and services while preserving the core, recognizable elements of AOL—its warmth and optimism.

In the original logo, the triangle contains two swirls moving in a closed circle. Here, the circle is transformed into a globe, an intuitive symbol of the benefits of the Internet: a roundtable where people come together; a circular,

never-ending power source; a trackball the user can always control; or even the center of the online universe around which new experiences orbit.

Gobé also gave the logo a three-dimensional quality, with rounded corners and corresponding highlights, which lifts it off of the background. Rounding the corners on the logo and the letterforms was critical to aligning the logo with the positioning—it's not about AOL, it's about the consumer.

"This is appropriate particularly when you consider that we live in a wireless society. We float in space and have the freedom to reach new dimensions. This logo also lives in space. It was a signal that the brand was moving into a new era," he adds.

Typography was updated with simple, light letterforms that convey warmth and modernity. The resulting signature is clean and well defined, and it stands out from competing logos on the Internet and in media space.

The finished logo projects the sense that AOL is the place where everything connects. It is the trailhead from which new experiences can be explored.

"It invites you in and takes you to different place," says Gobé.

Travelocity
Identity Design

Desgrippes Gobé, New York, New York

Like America Online, Travelocity was an early leader in its field—in its case, online travel planning. But before long, competitors such as Orbitz and Expedia began to infringe on its territory.

"Travelocity forgot that they were not in the technology business or simply providing tickets to people: They were in the business of providing dreams," says Desgrippes Gobé principal Marc Gobé.

Travelocity had a special edge that the others did not, however. Rather than simply list or describe a possible destination, the company actually sent representatives there to audit the location for specific criteria. The information the site provided was not a canned sales speech but rather a description that actually analyzed the destination.

This unique service gave customers a sense of trust in the company. Gobé wanted to build on that wedge. What was missing, however, was a real emotional connection to the brand. The old logo certainly didn't have it; its chartlike design could easily be mistaken for a financial group's mark.

Gobé's team began with an internal brainstorming session with Travelocity managers. The outcome was clear: Every person there had a real passion for the brand. They truly wanted it to be the best place for people to begin what would turn into wonderful travel experiences. The old brand did not speak of dreams or freedom or any of the things travelers anticipate.

The designers began by considering symbolism that would suggest dreams. The notion of wishing on a star—or wishing on many stars—emerged as a strong favorite.

"From an emotional perspective, we wanted the new logo to be more about possibilities. We wanted it to suggest that it can help you transcend your normal life. So we needed to express a sense of magic, discovery, imagination, freedom, and limitless boundaries," Gobé says.

The team's solution was a trio of loosely brushstroked stars. The hand-drawn effect makes the new logo more personal and friendly. Its simple nature complements the typography, which includes the company's slogan. Sans-serif type also feels friendly and approachable.

For color, the designers chose blue to signify open skies and orange to communicate energy. "Orange is an optimistic color," Gobé notes. "It's a transformative color, associated with the sun, so it is warm and glowing."

When used in reverse, the stars glow in white. "They give you the feeling you get when you lay down in a field at night: You can spend hours just looking at the sky and its mystery," he adds.

Working in tandem with Travelocity's new "spokes-gnome," the new logo literally changed the face of the business. The entire site adopted the same spirit as the logo. It is now more about discovery as opposed to just plopping information in front of the reader.

"The new identity reflects the desire of company employees to do a better job for people. It really shows their sincerity," the designer says.

Design Firm	Armstrong International CI
Client	2008 Olympics Committee
Project	Logo Design

The 2008 Beijing Olympics committee received 1,985 entries in response to its logo competition invitation, issued in 2002. Of these, 1,763 were from designers in China, Taiwan, and Hong Kong. Among the entries was work by designers who had won the logo competitions for the 1996 Atlanta Olympics, the 1998 Nagano Winter Olympics, the 2000 Sydney Olympics, and the 2002 Salt Lake City Winter Olympics.

Against this stiff competition, a design by Guo Chunning, president of Armstrong International Corporate Identity Design Co., Ltd. stood out. His logo portrays a running, celebrating figure—perfectly appropriate to the Games—but it has a distinct Chinese sensibility, plus plenty of hidden meaning.

> It has been more than 100 years since the Olympics were born, and now they have finally come to Beijing.

Among countries that might host the Olympics, China's history and culture are especially ancient and rich. It has many, many stories to share with the world. Creating a logo that picked out just the right stories and combining those with the spirit of the Olympics was challenging, says Guo.

"That was the problem we had to solve first," he says. "It has been more than 100 years since the Olympics were born, and now they finally come to Beijing. This is such a big honor."

Guo wanted to create a symbol that not only could be appreciated in nations and cultures around the world but also in the many subcultures of his own country.

"There were many, many cultural inheritances and artistic elements to consider—for instance, calligraphy, sculpture, silk, fresco, pottery and porcelain, religious art, folk art, and architectural arts. There were so many elements for us to choose from," he says.

After long consideration, Guo chose Chinese calligraphy and seal cutting. Still in use today, seal cutting is an ancient art that dates back 3,700 years. A seal is essentially a stamped signature produced intaglio with a carefully carved and thoughtfully designed stamp.

(Above) The logo for the 2008 Beijing Olympics was created by a Beijing design firm, Armstrong International Corporate Identity Design Co., Ltd. The design is built on the ancient Chinese art of seal cutting and on an actual Chinese character.

(Right) The design team began their explorations with this Chinese character, pronounced "jing." It means "Beijing," which is certainly appropriate, but in addition, the designers could see in it a human form that was running or leaping.

BEIJING 2008

(Above) The logo the team submitted to the Olympics Committee for consideration is basic in form. Because it uses red, the color traditionally used in the art of seal cutting, it has the appearance of a traditional seal cut stamp to those familiar to the art—generally, the Chinese host citizens. However, it also speaks to those who are not familiar with seal cutting.

(Right) The Olympic Committee asked that the Armstrong designers try out several typefaces. Traditional Western faces as well as Chinese brush-inspired faces were explored.

BEIJING 2008

修改方案之一

BEIJING 2008

修改方案之二

Beijing 2008

修改方案之三

Beijing 2008

修改方案之四

Beijing 2008

修改方案之五

Beijing 2008

修改方案之六

Beijing 2008

修改方案之七

Beijing 2008

修改方案之八

Beijing 2008

修改方案之九

Combining the figure and the color in the cutting turned it into an official seal of sorts.

(Top) Here, the character is modified to appear as if it is running or leaping. The sense of the Chinese character is still present, however. The trial at far right shows a child-lettered design; Armstrong asked 300 children to hand-write the words *Beijing 2008* in an attempt to capture a more unfettered spirit. Although they were appealing, none were chosen.

(Bottom) In this version, the running character changed yet again, although the type-face has been chosen: a simplified Chinese brush style.

The logo, called "Dancing Beijing," was released for use in 2003, and it now appears not only in Olympic and other athletic applications but also in signage and other graphics in its host city.

Guo and Armstrong chairman Zhang Wu also considered the relative success and appropriateness of logos from previous Games. Zhang felt that designs from the 1984, 1992, and 2004 Olympics were particularly successful.

Each Olympics logo represents the host country's culture and artistic characteristic, says Guo. He wanted Armstrong's logo to do the same, and more.

He began his design by selecting a Chinese character, pronounced "jing," meaning Beijing. This character is a very basic one, and through careful thought and experimentation, the designer was able to transform it into a pictograph of a running figure. To Guo, the figure represented the spirit of the Olympics: faster, higher, stronger.

> **The figure represented the spirit of the Olympics: faster, higher, stronger.**

"It is like a dancer waving his arms, welcoming friends from all over the world. It represents the new Beijing, a passionate Beijing, and an energetic Beijing," he says.

Guo decided to portray the figure in a seal cutting, which speaks of China's ancient culture and art. The color for seal cutting is red, which also happens to be the color of happiness and festival in the country. Combining the figure and the color in the cutting turned it into an official seal of sorts, but a seal that anyone around the world could understand. It made both the letterform and the art form universally understandable.

Selecting an appropriate typeface was a challenge. First, Guo tried a recognizable face, Times New Roman, as well as the face Chinese Brush. But neither of these had the same unfettered nature of Chinese calligraphy. So the design team invited 300 children to write, in their own handwriting, the words *Beijing 2008*. None of these trials was an ideal match, however, so finally Guo decided to use simplified Chinese brushstroked characters, which the Olympics committee praised.

The mark, called "Dancing Beijing," was released for use in 2003, and Zhang Wu and Guo are pleased with its life thus far.

"It is like my dream coming true," says Guo. "It was really hard to express my feelings in words at that time. I felt so proud that our Chinese design was well accepted by the world. This is a honor for my company, my country, and the Chinese designers."

China National Petroleum Corporation
Identity Design

Armstrong International CI, Beijing, China

The old logo of the China National Petroleum Corporation certainly did not reflect either the scope or the energy of the state holding company's main products, crude oil and natural gas. An oval, split lengthwise into yellow and red, featured the letters CNPC at its center.

There was little contrast between the letterforms and the yellow half of the logo, and that contrast all but disappeared when the logo was used small. When shown in combination with product logos from its own lines, it did not stand out. The company, which ranks forty-sixth in the Fortune Global 500 list, clearly needed a more distinctive identity.

CNPC asked Armstrong International Corporate Identity Design Co., Ltd. in Beijing, China, to build up its global image. To accomplish this, Armstrong director Zhang Wu and his team wanted to draw from the far more recognizable logo of a CNPC product, Kunlan lubricating oil.

"Kunlan Mountain is one of the most famous mountains in China. It has witnessed the development of Chinese civilization and is a significant visual element of Chinese civilization," says Zhang Wu.

The design team's solution combined the shape of the mountain with a rising sun, also a meaningful symbol in China, to form a round droplet shape. "It is like an oil drop, representing the ambition of CNPC," the director explains. "It represents never-ending energy, the motto of CNPC—'Dedication to the energy industry, building the harmony'—the relationship between CNPC and the [Chinese] people, and between CNPC and nature."

Maintaining the original color scheme made sense: The colors are warm, consistent with the company's dedication to building harmony, and red and yellow are the colors of the Chinese national flag. While yellow was ineffective as a background for letters in the original logo, it works well as a backdrop to a rising sun.

The new logo has been well received, and it is quickly being disseminated inside and outside the country. It has traveled to Antarctica with a Chinese team of researchers sponsored by CNPC. In addition, the corporation is an official sponsor of the 2008 Beijing Olympics, so its new identity will soon be visible to people worldwide.

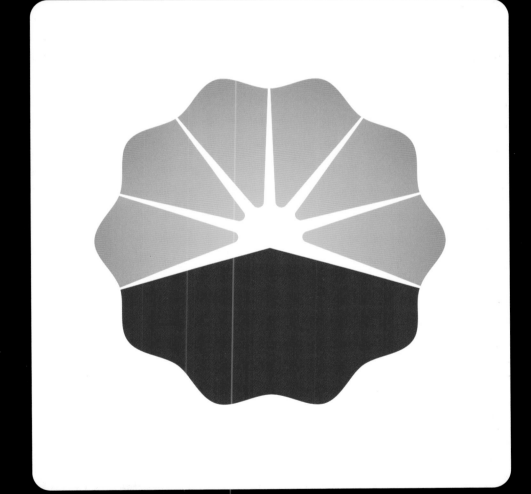

Design Firm	Lippincott Mercer
Client	Bank of New York
Project	Corporate Identity Redesign

A client with a 200-year history also has 200 years' worth of identity, for better or for worse. That's what Lippincott Mercer discovered when it began to excavate the brand identity of the Bank of New York.

The Bank of New York's logo—a safe burgundy box with white type inside—had been a regional icon, long recognizable in the New York area but uninspiring just the same. In the mid-1990s, the Bank embarked on a ten-year string of acquisitions. More than eighty acquisitions later, the bank had vastly broadened its capabilities in custody, trade execution and clearing, corporate trust, and institutional asset management. No longer a regional entity, the Bank needed to be reintroduced to the world.

> A big part of reintroducing the Bank of New York, which was founded by Alexander Hamilton, was implementing a new identity.

"Founded by Alexander Hamilton, the Bank of New York is America's oldest bank. In fact, it was the first bank in the colonies to create currency," explains Alex de Janosi, lead designer for the project at Lippincott Mercer. "It has an incredibly rich history. But it has grown considerably in the last fifteen to twenty-five years. Today, it moves a trillion dollars a day."

The Bank has always had a large retail footprint, but customers, both individuals and corporate entities, did not realize how much it had changed. Even Bank of New York employees did not fully understand the new scope. The Bank had become a leading provider of financial services on an international level. A big part of reintroducing the financial giant was implementing a new identity.

"The Bank's old logo was very drab, very dated. It was nothing horrible, but certainly nothing evocative," explains de Janosi. Trite images of globes, meant to suggest a global presence, also figured prominently in Bank promotions. Most collateral materials were printed on uninspiring cream-colored stock.

Even more troublesome, the burgundy box logo was used inconsistently. "Every line of business that the Bank of New York had could do whatever it wanted. Everything was disparate and not uniform. We needed to make 'the Bank of New York' the brand here, not the company's different offerings and products."

(Above) The Bank of New York's new logo, designed by Lippincott Mercer, radiates the power and dynamism of the organization while quietly noting its 200-year history.

(Right) The client's old logo was safe but uninspiring and even drab in many applications. In addition, the Bank's many divisions used the identity inconsistently.

The new mark is embossed for special applications, such as executive business cards.

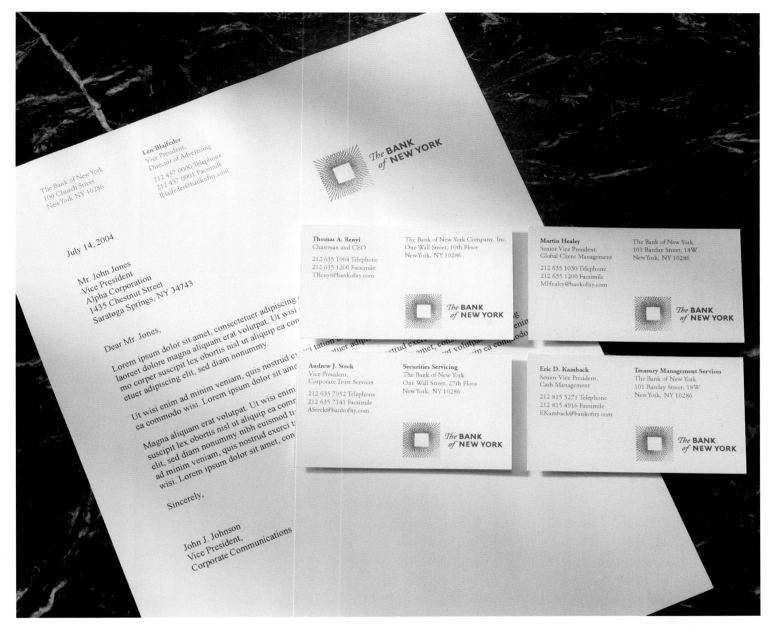

Color and pattern make the Bank of New York's new logo an enormous leap forward in terms of presence in the market. The patterning in the logo references traditional patterning in currency and financial certificates, while the colors suggest the modern world and its energetic pace. The empty center of the new mark could even be regarded as a subtle mimic of the original square mark.

The logo isn't a beauty mark; it has to convey specific attributes.

Lippincott Mercer's job was threefold:

- Organize the Bank's many divisions, business, and offerings so future marketing efforts could be integrated.

- Create a new marketing platform.

- Create a new identity program that, at a glance, helps customers understand the Bank of New York.

Lippincott Mercer began the project by interviewing the Bank's key audiences, including banking professionals, employees, clients, and financial analysts, to better understand wider perceptions of the brand, especially in relation to how competitors (such as State Street, Mellon, and JP Morgan Chase) were regarded.

After a year of research, the design team identified a clear set of brand attributes, which included descriptors such as *responsive, industry leader,* and *global.*

"As designers, we don't put pencil to paper until the attributes are agreed upon. The logo isn't a beauty mark; it has to convey specific attributes," de Janosi says.

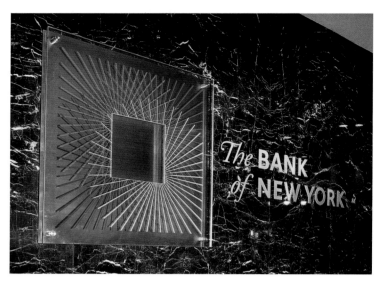

The levels of radiating lines in the mark are especially useful in dimensional applications, such as this signage.

> To balance the bright colors and flowing lines, the team crafted solid, stable typography.

Eight designers then began creating a broad range of symbols and logotypes. This marked a surprisingly lengthy phase of the project. Nearly six months passed, during which the client even considered abandoning the Bank of New York name.

During the exploration process, the designers looked at images of Alexander Hamilton's financial motifs, graphic patterns and shapes, and straight typographic expressions.

The design team met with the project director to narrow the hundreds of marks to a list of ten ideas to present to the Bank's chairman.

The designers had discovered shapes and overlapping lines that resembled engraving patterns on historic stock certificates and global currencies. The intertwining lines suggested the Bank's comprehensive and integrated array of services.

The response by the client was favorable. "They really liked the idea of graphics that expressed transactions, management, and movement of money," de Janosi says.

When an early sample of the patterning concept was shown together with other ideas, the Bank of New York chair and other members of top management rallied around it. The ebb and flow of the linear patterning spoke to the Bank's technical abilities. The introduction of transparent colors gave the mark a fresh, modern look while conveying an established, elegant feel, plus the square shape of the design subtly referenced the shape of the old logo.

To balance the bright colors and flowing lines, de Janosi's team crafted solid, stable typography. The logotype, a combination of the fonts Bliss and Adobe Garamond, was carefully customized: Ligatures between the *T* and *he* as the elegant italic of *the* and *of* represent the history of the brand. The elegant gray of the type balances well with the vibrant linework in the mark, nicely mixing history with modernity.

The visual equity of the original logo's box was maintained. The shape is called "the jewel box." It is as if the original burgundy box were opened and all the colorful workings of the company revealed. The shape of the box is echoed in the design grid used in many other applications today— the Bank's website, signage, and more.

De Janosi and his team worked many hours making certain that the line weights involved with the jewel box were appropriate and that lines inside related to the bounding box correctly. Of course, there were many production aspects to consider with the fine lines and choice of colors.

"With a five-color logo, anything can get mangled in the wrong hands. But the internal marketing staff at the Bank runs a tight ship, and they keep a close eye on how people use the jewel box. It's an ongoing job."

Although at the start of the project, the Bank of New York had many fiefdoms that each had a strong opinion about the company's identity and its use. Today, the many divisions have embraced the new look and philosophy.

The Bank of New York's new look is a definite swing away from the past as well as a shift away from the personality of competitors. It's even more successful than de Janosi originally believed it might be.

"The culture of the previous identity was weighed down with yellow-cream paper, burgundy boxes, and so on. I was surprised at senior management's excitement over the new mark, which we presented as a real long shot. They were all over it," he recalls. "The lesson for me is to not underestimate a client's tastes or capabilities. The client can see beauty and function just the same as you do."

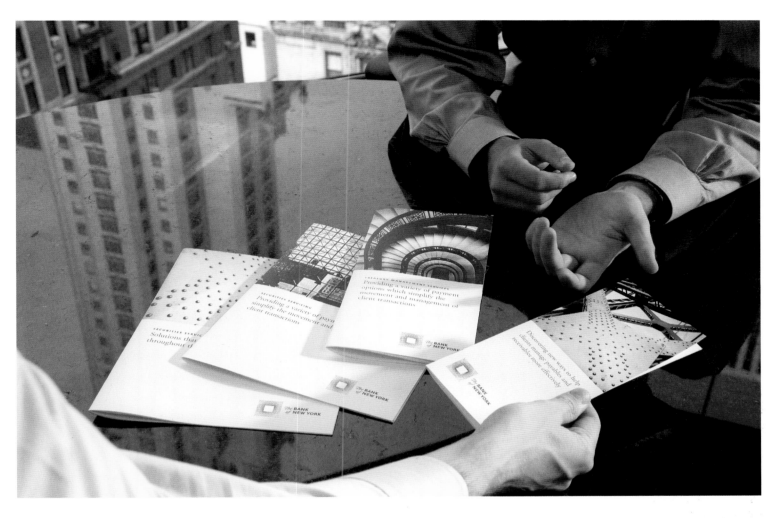

(Top) The shape of the new logo drives a grid system that is easily adaptable for collateral design.

(Bottom) Because of its mix of modern and traditional, the new logo is extremely flexible. It can be used in applications small and large.

Sprint
Identity Design

Lippincott Mercer, New York, New York

The goal in developing a new identity for the company formed by the 2005 merger of Sprint and Nextel was to retain valuable visual equities from each company yet move on to a stronger, even more valuable positioning. Even though the new company would be named Sprint, its new management team did not want to suggest that one company was overpowering the other. This was to be a real merger.

"We wanted to explore the 'Sprintness' and 'Nextelness' the identity needed, as well as the ramifications for creating something in a completely new direction," explains Rodney Abbot, senior partner at Lippincott Mercer (New York City), the design and brand consultancy that developed the new Sprint logo. "We had to retain what was valuable from both brands and move forward, not just move on."

The original Sprint organization had come to own such concepts as clarity—as portrayed by the famous pin drop—as well as dynamism and the heritage of a friendly communications business. Nextel owned the color combination of yellow and black in the communications market. Combined with a direct, no-nonsense attitude, its original logo felt solid and technologically strong.

Abbot and his design team developed many directions. Some stayed close to the original identities, while others signaled a complete break from the past. All the designs were created to convey the key brand qualities of choice, flexibility, clarity, immediacy, directness, and straight talk.

"We wanted to visually express the experience the customer would have, regardless of whether the customer is a business or personal use customer," says Abbot. The new logo had to communicate the company's appropriate connection to home and business.

As their design work progressed, the team noted that the most emotional responses from focus groups were garnered from simple, direct, strong shapes, those that had a dynamic sense of movement and a distinct personality. The final design captured those qualities and expressed them in a new design reminiscent of a wing. It has a quality of flight, freedom, and movement, especially when it is run in the familiar Nextel yellow.

"It also has a sense of moving forward," Abbot says. "It indicates a transformation in the communication experience you will have with the new brand."

For the type, the designers selected a sans serif that felt fresher and more responsive than the Garamond Italic used in the old Sprint logo and the heavy sans used in the old Nextel logo. Open letterspacing allows the new symbol to fly untethered.

Design Firm	FutureBrand
Client	Brand Australia
Project	Corporate Identity Redesign

No one would deny that Australia is an exotic, fantastic vacation destination. Trouble is, it's quite a hike from just about everywhere else in the world: A traveler makes a considerable effort to get there. Given, in addition, the SARS scare in Southeast Asia and the general nervous malaise caused by terrorism worldwide, visits to Australia declined in 2003.

At that time, the Australian Tourism Commission decided to refresh the country's tourism identity and rejuvenate travelers' interest. The commission itself was rebranded as Tourism Australia, and the new group came to FutureBrand with a challenging brief.

> The goal: Create a 360-degree view of Australia by aligning key ideas and messages across policy, trade, and travel channels.

First, they wanted to refresh Brand Australia's visual image and create a 360-degree view of Australia by aligning key ideas and messages across policy, trade, and travel channels. The new identity had to establish a comprehensive brand strategy that would help partners like Qantas, the Australian airline, and state tourism authorities work in a more complementary way. Finally, the new identity system had to be flexible so that partners—in tourism, education, trade, and politics—could enjoy success through the use of the same smart branding tools.

"The client's old identity did not reflect how Australia had emerged as a major destination. There is a rich, deep story here to be told," explains Ken Shadbolt, creative director of FutureBrand's Melbourne office.

Shadbolt's designers were presented with a brief informed by New York–based brand consultancy Brand Architecture International:

- The Australian experience is bright, literally and figuratively, which cultivates a pervasive and infectious candor and optimism.

- It is a place that lives in the future tense, always looking and creating forward, where time is always now.

- Australia is a place refreshingly free of boundaries, inhibitions, and constraints, where "having a go" is still possible.

(Above) Show Australia in a different light—that was the goal of the FutureBrand team in designing a new identity for Australia.com. The jumping kangaroo, the distinctive typeface and color palette, indigenous patterning, and, perhaps most distinctive, the glow or flare or spark of the sun all play an important part of the design solution.

(Right) The old identity spoke clearly of sun, sea, and life native to Australia, but it was somewhat uninspiring and flat. It did not tell the viewer anything about the experiences he or she might have there.

• It is a place where blue-sky thinking is the rule, not the exception.

• It is a place in which one cannot help but be irreverent, to approach things from unexpected angles, to see things through different lenses.

"A different light" was a leading factor from the start of the project, says Shadbolt. The concept referred to the actual physical quality of the light in Australia as well as the country's sense of can-do energy and optimism. "People often comment when they step off a plane that they are quite struck by the intensity of light, its vibrancy," he says. "We wanted to capture that vibrancy as well as the effect it has on all living things that are touched by it."

The challenge for the FutureBrand team was to find a way to express visually this physical and emotional light. Their ideas came from many sources. They looked at photos that contained evocative light phenomena, such as sunbursts, flares, reflections on water, refraction, and backlighting. Because of the country's reputation for wonderful sun and water, these could all be used in the new identity.

Any photography used as part of the identity, they decided, should deliberately avoid typical tourist shots. Many of the images in the previous photographic library showed beautiful landscapes at sunset, but they were all shot with the sun behind the photographer. "We wanted to challenge that predictable approach," says Shadbolt. Instead, the FutureBrand team decided to commission photography from a more unusual angle—directly into the sun—making the images considerably more distinctive.

Vibrant light inspiration also came from the charged strokes of contemporary indigenous art. "The living line," the designers called it, as it is full of shimmering dots and swirling shapes that are full of energy and indeed, history. Lines, they reasoned, could symbolize feelings and patterns of energy.

"Bringing these graphics to the fore of this identity system was very important," says Shadbolt. "We commissioned an indigenous group—Balarinji, based in Sydney—to create this artwork. We briefed them to explore art that expressed emotional states, such as calmness or adventure. We were so excited when the work came back. The extraordinary connection between the land and the people who live here is beautifully expressed by this artwork."

(Above) The colors and patterning of Australian indigenous art play an important part in the finished identity. The graphical patterning can be run over photos or used as dividers or incidental art.

(Below) The designers created a palette of five colors, each with two shades—one as the color appears in full sun and one as it appears in shade. Some combinations were lively, suggesting adventure. Others were more grounded to suggest the rest and peace travelers also desire from a vacation destination. All the colors emerged from the native surroundings of the country.

The colors used in the indigenous art, photography, and other applications were crucial to the identity's success. The designers built a distinctive palette of five colors, each with two shades—one as the color appears in full sun, the other as it appears in shadow. Some could be used in what they called "irreverent combinations" to suggest the excitement of travel and adventure. Others made more "grounded" pairs, perfect for representing the peace and quiet space travelers also seek from their experiences abroad.

Two contrasting typefaces were selected for the project. FutureBrand worked with the Font Bureau to customize an existing hand-drawn font for brief applications, such as headlines and call-outs, that can have more personality. These typefaces were complemented by a relaxed and straightforward sans-serif font used for informational text.

> We decided to work with the roo—it was pretty much a given. However, the way we represented it had to be very distinctive.

The design team carefully studied what competing tourist destinations, such as Hawaii, Brazil, Japan, Spain, Malaysia, New Zealand, and others, were doing. They also considered the recognizable icons of Australia, including the kangaroo from the original identity.

"From an Australian perspective, the kangaroo is a bit of a cliché. Most of us are so affected by clichés that we immediately want to get rid of them. However, when you think about someone in another part of the world who is considering five to ten possible locations to visit, we have to cut through quickly with our message. The unique shape of the kangaroo carries considerable equity of Australia," says Shadbolt. "The old version of the kangaroo was quite tired. As we were reminded of many times during this identity refresh, there are no tired icons, just tired expressions."

The kangaroo, in addition to building on existing equity (within the commission and with businesses such as Qantas) and being a highly recognizable icon, is also a living creature with the same irrepressible spirit that the new commission wanted to express. The animal in the previous logo seemed to be on a downward trajectory. For the new logo, the designers experimented with showing the kangaroo on an upward journey. Many drawings also showed a sun with just a suggestion of a smile.

Their final design includes the leaping animal, a sun drawn in a loose style, colors that sweep from high noon to dusk, spirited typography, and a sunburst or flare of light.

"We decided to work with the roo—it was pretty much a given. However, the way we represented it had to be distinctive. We made it come alive with the light. The light gets in and affects you. The spirit can't be dormant here," says Shadbolt.

An additional benefit of the new logo and identity system is that it is very flexible: all of its components can be mixed and matched in endless

Two new fonts were created for a hand-drawn and casual look. One is used for short applications, such as headlines, and one for informational text, as shown here.

The kangaroo might be an Australian cliché, but it is so firmly connected to the country that it is impossible to ignore. The key to using it smartly is to give it special life and energy, just like the country itself. These are just a few of the roos that auditioned for the starring role in the identity.

combinations. For instance, a pattern can be used alone on top of color, or it can serve as a transitional element between a block of solid color and a photo. A pattern can be overlaid on a photo, which always yields a wonderful play of light and people. The emphasis is on demonstrating that the Australian experience involves much more than just seeing icons. It is about feeling the whole of the place.

Implemented in May 2004, the new system is being credited with an increase in attention. At the end of December 2004, international tourist traffic into Australia was up 9 percent from the previous year, and it increased by a further 7 percent in the nine months to September 2005.

The Brand Council in the United Kingdom has named Australia as one of the world's Cool BrandLeaders, especially interesting as this is the first time a country was included on this annual list. Additionally, in November 2005 Australia was awarded the title of "best worldwide country," by readers of the *Sunday Times* Travel Magazine in the United Kingdom.

"Our brand identity work has played its part in communicating Brand Australia more clearly and consistently around the world," says Shadbolt, "so it's hard to argue with the notion that multidimensional brands like countries really benefit from careful thought in the expression of their offer."

"Our job was to inspire tourism, but this identity also affects other areas of trade. Other Australian organizations are looking at leveraging the new identity in a much broader role internationally. One possibility is that, over time, it will become the national brand," says Shadbolt.

Australia has many well photographed sites and sights. Rather than rely on these alone, as so many did before, the designers decided to add two more elements: the unusual quality of light presented by the Australian sun, and the human element. The latter helps viewers imagine themselves in the picture. In the samples above, indigenous patterning is also played over the photo, enhancing the sense of the fantastic. In the samples at right, patterning is used in combination with color as a graphic divider.

The new logo and identity system is enormously flexible. Color, light, fonts, patterns, and photos can be combined in endless ways.

More samples of printed pieces. Note how the distinctive quality of light shines through in each photo and how patterning adds layer, dimension, and personality to the other elements.

2006 Commonwealth Games
Identity Design

FutureBrand, Melbourne, Australia

Like the Olympic Games, the Commonwealth Games bring together talented athletes and enthusiastic fans every four years. Also like the Olympic Games, the Commonwealth Games have a different host city and different logo and identity each time they are held. Unlike the Olympic Games, though, the Commonwealth Games are open only to countries in the British Commonwealth, which makes them a much more intimate event. Without the power countries that tend to dominate the Olympic Games, many more Commonwealth athletes have a chance to demonstrate their personal best.

MELBOURNE
2006
XVIII COMMONWEALTH GAMES   TM©

FutureBrand Melbourne, which designed the identity for the 2000 Summer Olympic Games in Sydney, Australia, had clear ideas about where it wanted to take the 2006 Commonwealth Games logo. Past logos had a strong British flavor: in fact, right into the 1970s and 1980s, they almost all contained a reference to the Union Jack. The past marks also felt formal, with no sense of the celebration and thrill the athletes and audiences experience.

"We really wanted to cut free of the British ties," explains Ken Shadbolt, creative director of FutureBrand. "It is the games of the Commonwealth, but what is the relevance of that to the games today? For us, it meant the notion of diverse backgrounds and origins, but of shared values."

At the outset of the project, the FutureBrand team discovered it would have to incorporate the Commonwealth Federation logo—just created—into the Games logo. Having worked with the Olympic rings, the designers knew that the federation mark would have to be prominent despite its lack of graphic inspiration.

Unlike Sydney, Melbourne does not have physical icons that are recognized worldwide, which was an additional complication. The city does, however, have a cultural sophistication the designers felt they could express visually. The new logo could be a celebration of sport and culture together.

"These games are all about youthful optimism and sportsmanship, but more about taking part than winning. We wanted to communicate a sense of celebration beyond the sport, because actually, many cultural events run concurrently to the games. So the new symbol would have to represent those experiences as well," says Shadbolt.

The solution expresses the spirit of athleticism and celebration, of diverse origins and colors, and of sharing. Two figures mesh, one striving and one celebrating, and together form a hint of an M. This logo celebrates winning not just through actual victory but through sportsmanship and experience as well.

Shadbolt feels the new logo raises the excitement of the event several notches and will give future designers expanded license in future logo designs. The project will open up over time, and, like the Olympic Games, give both future athletes and designers splendid opportunities.

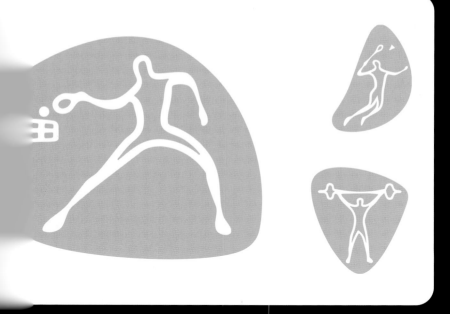

Design Firm	Wolff Olins
Client	Beeline
Project	Corporate Identity System

The cell and mobile phone market is growing explosively around the world, including Russia, where a number of providers are already in place. The number-two player in early 2005 was Beeline, a brand that had been in existence since 1993. Beeline had the same serious business problem as other providers: a sizable hole in its client loyalty quotient. Seventy percent of Muscovites use cell phones, and most were selecting their cell service strictly on the basis of price. They were easily distracted by newer and cheaper options.

Brand loyalty—and, indeed, the concept of a brand—was little known. Beeline wanted to find a way to secure an invaluable emotional tie to their customers: it needed a recognizable brand.

> Brand loyalty—and, indeed, the concept of a brand—was little known at Beeline.

Beeline's competition, which included MTC and Megaphone, was tough, but Beeline had the benefit of an already well-recognized logo, which contained a bee. The old logo represented the brand name in Cyrillic letters, with the image of the bee between "Bee" and "line" against a blue background. It was a naïve but compelling and friendly icon, something the creative team at Wolff Olins, which was asked to create the new brand, could build around.

The Wolff Olins creative team was asked to keep the heritage bumblebee in the final design solution. It carried some brand equity and had a real sense of life. Moreover, because bees are known for building communities, collaborating, and communicating, the image held particular relevance for the client.

But the designers considered a less literal take on the bee. Rather than include the image of an actual bee in the new logo, they decided to appropriate its yellow and black striped pattern.

"We wanted to give Beeline something they could own and play with graphically—something recognizable, free, and inspiring," explains Marina Willer, Wolff Olins creative director for the project.

The striped pattern became a theme that could be applied to almost anything—clothing, objects, even other animals. Some of Willer's favorite applications have been a zebra and ice cream: "Because they twist

(Above) Wolff Olins designers took the identity of the cell phone company Beeline from drab to full of personality and color. The new logo stands out by virtue of its simplicity.

(Right) Beeline's original logo suggested energy and communication, but its main character, the bee, did not have much life. Amid the cacophony of talk and marketing that surrounds the competitive Russian cell phone market, it just did not stand out.

escape

create

Rather than play out Beeline's new logo over and over, the Wolff Olins design team applied the mark's distinctive color scheme to everyday objects that suggested inspirational messages such as escape or relax. As these signboards show, neither the logo nor the company name must be shown to communicate the brand.

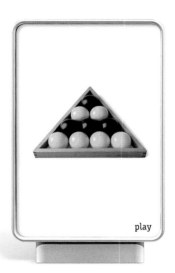

play

live life

dream

relax

ordinary images that people are familiar with into something extraordinary, that treatment makes them Beeline and nothing else."

Yellow is an energetic, warm color, and this quality made the new identity appealing to Russians. "With the weather and history there, Russia can be a tough place to live. It's almost surreal. I think people are desperate for sun and warmth. The contrast with black is quite brutal, but it works there. Subtlety is something that would just not work," Willer says.

> We wanted to provide a breath of fresh air with plenty of white space.

When Wolff Olins began working with Beeline in mid-2005, the idea of a branded experience was not widely known in Russia. "The notion of a consistent brand across several media is new in Russia," says Willer. "Big cities like Moscow have a busy, noisy landscape. Everything is big, and there is a lot of noise pollution. Everyone is shouting their marketing message at the same volume. It really is a brutal landscape."

A metropolitan city like London or New York City is also quite loud, she notes, but these cities regulate and limit the size and placement of billboards and other visual media. Russian cities have no such rules. This environment was quite a concern for the design team when they first arrived. How could Beeline even begin to be noticed?

"That's when we decided to do something quite simple. We wanted to provide a breath of fresh air with plenty of white space," says Willer.

All of Beeline's marketing messages are surrounded with clean, empty space, an effect that is remarkable in the crowded urban landscape. Only one or two images are used with each message, and few words. Willer says this approach required the client to be brave because it runs counter to so many conventions of normally riotous Russian advertising.

"The client has been passionate about developing this brand. They really understand the need for creating a brand that cuts through the clutter," she adds.

Beeline always had fair prices, so it was respected by customers. But since the new brand began buzzing, more customers have begun to give the company their loyalty. Beeline has moved from being trusted to being loved. The new brand is meant to inspire and encourage people, to open up new horizons of thought.

Beeline now has one distinct message, not many, says Willer. Customers understand and respond to that.

Another important part of the new Beeline identity is the use of plenty of white space. That attribute alone makes the company's messaging entirely unlike its competitors'.

Beeline has moved from being trusted to being loved. The new brand is meant to inspire and encourage people, to open up new horizons of thought.

Unilever
Identity Design

Wolff Olins, London, United Kingdom

Consumers around the world choose Unilever products 150 million times every day, yet most of them are unaware of it. Unilever is a blue-chip company by any standard, but as a brand it is almost invisible in most Western countries.

By the time Wolff Olins began working with Unilever, in early 2002, the decision had been made to make more of the Unilever brand. The first task was to articulate what the business stood for, something that could be an anchor and touchstone for Unilever in the future. "The idea was that Unilever adds vitality to life," explains Lee Coomber, Wolff Olins creative director for Unilever's new identity project.

"The idea of vitality gives everyone in Unilever a shared sense of purpose. It suggests a new way of thinking and behaving, and it guides the organization's crucial investment and innovation decisions. Importantly, it also drives Unilever's program for social and environmental responsibility."

Unilever's existing logo suggested a steel company rather than something that felt vital or that consumers would put on or in their body.

The design team did not feel a reductionist logo would be a good fit for such a rich and diverse company. "No other company covers everything from household cleaner to fish fingers—no one else has the breadth of product. Another thing to consider was that the company has always had strong values in terms of the environment, in terms of being beneficial," Coomber says.

The designers wanted to celebrate this by representing the three main areas—people, products, and the environment—and so created twenty-five icons, each with a tie to at least one of the three categories. For example, a fish is a symbol of food but also of the environment. A palm tree represents paradise for people in northern climates, but it represents a staple food crop to some in southern realms.

Combining these icons into one symbol, the letter U, the design team created a demonstrative logo that tells a rich story of the company. Its complexity flies in the face of most logo design theory, but the simple letterform makes it work, even when print applications are less than ideal.

The new logo, although it is based on a letterform from the alphabet—the one used to write English—still has international appeal because of its simple shape. Even better, Coomber reports that audiences around the world see different messages in it, messages that feel personal.

"Some people say it looks like a henna tattoo. Some see Delft pottery. Other people see something aboriginal. That pleased us enormously," he says.

Design Firm	Turner Duckworth
Client	Brains Brewing
Project	Identity/Packaging Redesign

The name of the largest independent brewer in Wales sounds odd to any-one outside the region: Brains. This family name has been on the business since 1882. The brewery now operates about 250 pubs, where it serves its traditional beers to very loyal customers.

In 2004, the company faced this situation: it wanted to preserve and enhance customer loyalty but absolutely had to connect with its newest employees. These employees had worked for a number of smaller regional breweries Brains had purchased, and like many people in this situation, they felt disheartened and disenfranchised.

> The old Brains logo was much like that found at other traditional British pubs.

Brains management wanted to create a positive experience for everyone, customers and employees alike. It also wanted to reflect a sense of national pride, which was on the upswing in Wales.

"Cardiff, the capital of Wales, has had a big upsurge in its fortunes," explains Bruce Duckworth of Turner Duckworth, the design firm tapped by Brains to redesign its logo and identity. "Traditionally, Cardiff had a mining culture. Today, the city is coming back to the forefront with a new opera house, a Welsh Assembly Building, and its own governmental buildings. There really is a sense of renewed national pride."

The old Brains logo was much like that found at other traditional British pubs—an almost stereotypical crest from long ago. It did, however, include a dragon, a positive and patriotic symbol also found on the Welsh flag.

"We thought the logo looked medieval, like a coat of arms," recalls Duck-worth. "The dragon is the national symbol of Wales, so it is an appropriate symbol. But this one looked old. The curly chain effect underneath is par-ticularly medieval."

The creative team decided to keep the dragon but reconsidered it in a con-temporary light. How could the symbol be made more relevant for today? Dragons are all about fire and aggression, but the original dragon looked a bit passive. Even more, he was walking in the wrong direction.

Brains Brewery is a venerable company with a brand-new logo, compliments of Turner Duckworth, London and San Francisco. The new identity is decidedly traditional but has plenty of con-temporary flair.

The original Brains identity was relatively innocuous. Its dragon was flat, not fierce; its typography was generic; and, after many decades, its chain element had become meaningless.

The Turner Duckworth team had to respect the original logo, but they also wanted to create a mark that customers and employees—some of whom had just been brought into the Brains fold through acquisitions—could all get behind. The dragon was a heraldic symbol, but the designers felt they could make it more modern. Turning the creature to the forward-facing position also improved the design. The chain could be deleted, but its color could be reused, as these trials show.

This comparison of the old (left) and new (right) dragons shows how much the animal was changed. The new version is prouder and more highly dimensional.

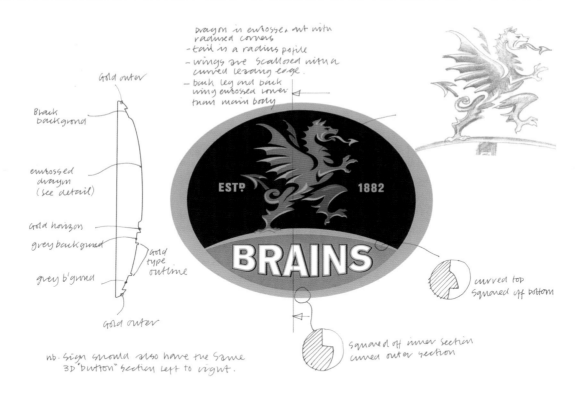

This logo had to make employees and citizens feel proud.

All heraldry symbols, like the dragon and chain, had high significance at one time. So the creative team consulted extensively with coats-of-arms experts to make sure that turning the dragon around wouldn't be a graphic faux pas. They discovered that at one time the direction the dragon faced on a knight's shield indicated whether he was right- or left-handed. But that significance was certainly no longer relevant.

The chain element, once representative of a piece of cloth around the base of a knight's helmet, also no longer had meaning. It could be deleted or reworked.

The first change the designers made was to make the dragon face and walk to the right—forward, so to speak. They also made the creature look prouder and gave it more personality, whereas the previous dragon was flatly generic.

Although the team played with modern interpretations of the chain element underneath the dragon, this was ultimately replaced with a smooth, golden horizon line that emphasized the forward motion of the creature.

"The dragon is more heroic now. He is leaning forward, striving, coming up over a golden horizon. He also has flecks and highlights of gold that add to his dimension," Duckworth says.

The client liked the design that shows the dragon coming over a golden horizon. To test the design in context, the Turner Duckworth designers applied it to various elements that would be seen in and around a pub, including signage and tap handles (right). They also drew up specs for signage that accentuated the dimensionality of the design.

The typography, too, was changed extensively. Rather than use a predictable and generic serif face, the designers created a more ownable, hand-drawn sans serif that curves in relationship with the horizon line. It is much more modern and strong, and, when used separately from the dragon, is still readily identifiable as a Brains symbol.

The entire creative team was pleased with the outcome, as were the people at Brains. "Sometimes we are asked to do a logo and are aware that we are really just freshening things up. But this logo had a lot more to do—to make employees and citizens feel proud," says Duckworth. "All the new employees in the new operation have a new logo they recognize as theirs."

Duckworth says that since the new identity has been in use, sales have increased 28 percent: "Not bad for a product that has been around for over 100 years," he adds.

The new design has enormous presence and reflects the pride of its region of origin, Cardiff, Wales. The typography is also modern and strong. It is an identity that employees are proud to claim, especially on the jerseys of professional football players.

Heavenly
Identity Design

Turner Duckworth, London, United Kingdom

Heavenly is a new brand with a mission: to launch products of all sorts and donate a portion of sales to nonprofit organizations. Heavenly embraces the concept of embedded giving—that is, as consumers get, they give. The company asked Turner Duckworth to create a logo for its brand that could work across many disparate products, from cafés to insurance to wine.

Heavenly was ready to launch its first product, an online wine store that sells more than 300 brands of fine wine, plus its own wine as well. The embedded giving for this product donates to Water Aid, which provides clean water for the world's poorest people. When you purchase the product, you literally can change wine to water, says Bruce Duckworth, principal of Turner Duckworth, the design office that created Heavenly's new identity.

"The most important thing was to give the name *Heavenly* a meaning that had nothing to do with heaven," laughs Duckworth in his London office. The brand was not meant to allude to anything religious, or, even worse, to sound pompous or pious. Heavenly was more of an adverb, as in being able to help other people while you are enjoying a good wine or other high-quality product. "Sounds heavenly, doesn't it?"

The Turner Duckworth designers experimented with four approaches, all meant to convey heavenly yet down-to-earth thinking and attitude, Duckworth says. The first design involved using the word *heavenly* as a suffix to just about anything:

"a good cup of tea...Heavenly"; "a great ice-cold vodka...Heavenly"; or even "hassle-free insurance... Heavenly." This concept could also be expressed in shorthand, more of a logo, as just "...h."

Another design used three little characters to deliver a familiar message: "Hear, see, and speak no evil." Heavenly was all about its straightforward method—a brand that cut through the marketing rubbish that prevents customers from understanding products. "They don't flower up their message," Duckworth says.

A third concept used a downward-pointing bracket to communicate the idea of benefit coming from heaven. The design that eventually won starts with this thought and makes it into a strong, singular logo featuring a lowercase h with a five-pointed star beneath it. The negative space between these two elements creates a downward-pointing arrow, bringing heaven down to Earth. This formed a logo that was both ownable and meaningful for the client.

Heavenly, still a fledgling company, is using its new identity on its first brand, heavenly wine (www.heavenlywine.co.uk). The logo works well, Duckworth says, because it represents the attitude of the company in a distinctive and simple way rather than relating to a particular product. Heavenly can go into many diverse areas and still use the same logo, because its ethos of embedded giving will always be relevant.

...heavenly

HEAVENLY
DOWN TO EARTH CONSULTANCY

heavenly™

marketing

heavenlyvodka

ice cold
pure russian
vodka...
heavenly

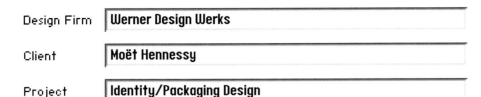

Design Firm	Werner Design Werks
Client	Moët Hennessy
Project	Identity/Packaging Design

10 Cane is a high-end, light amber-colored clear rum made from the first press of a new sugarcane crop. It is a liquor made for mixing with fresh juices, fruit, other liquor—or, of course, Coke. But it is not meant for everyday drinks; it might be purchased for home consumption, but 10 Cane is much more likely to be enjoyed mixed into a $10 cocktail at a trendy club, says Sharon Werner of Werner Design Werks, Minneapolis. Her firm was hired by distiller Moët Hennessy to name and create an identity for the then-unnamed rum in 2003.

"It's a rum for people who want the best rum and Coke they have ever had, the kind of cocktail that Ernest Hemingway would have ordered, the classic cocktail," says Werner.

> 10 Cane is a rum for people who want the best rum and Coke they have ever had.

The fact that the rum can be produced only when the new cane crop is ready automatically makes it an expensive product, about $40 per liter. Its exotic, exclusive origin and traditional brewing process make it unique, almost alchemic.

"The client wanted to play into the mixology and alchemy of a cocktail. This rum fit because it is made in a very old way but produced as a contemporary luxury brand. The alchemy was there, so the identity had to have the same feel," Werner says.

Prior to Werner Design's work on the project, Moët Hennessy had worked with Fallon Brand Consulting to determine the feasibility of the brand. Fallon spent a year determining who would buy the rum and how they would drink it. The firm's findings ran counter to the notion of a "spring break rum," which might be consumed not only in great quantity but also in fruity, sugary drinks.

This new brand was far more restrained. It had to feel modern enough to mix in easily at the club scene but also look as if it had been around for a long time, Werner says. "Our target customer was a twenty-three- to thirty-five-year-old male you might see at the airport with a beat-up but highest-quality briefcase. He has comfortable but high-quality clothing, a vintage Rolex, and an iPod. He is comfortable with traveling and flying. He probably has everything he needs for two weeks in a small carry-on. The brand had to be like that—not trying overly hard to impress."

10 Cane is a high-end rum, meant to stand out in an elegant way in trendy clubs. Werner Design Werks created its identity and packaging, an alchemic mix of old and new.

To communicate that 10 Cane is a new product made using an age-old recipe, designers Sharon Werner and Sarah Nelson at first considered a flask bottle design. This idea was eventually discarded because of production concerns, but the design of the crest-like logo combined with a modern paper label was retained.

(Above) This sloped-shoulder bottle is plain but classic. Its long neck, covered with texture, makes it stand out on the crowded bar shelf and is easy for bartenders to grip.

(Left) Imprinting a heraldic crest on the bottle gave it an aged look. Elements include monkeys, foliage, sugarcane, and engraved currency. But the addition of the warm orange paper label—various trials are shown here—gives the design contemporary confidence.

The new name not only refers to the main ingredient but also has the sense of an age-old recipe.

Werner and Nelson also experimented with color combinations. The key was to make the viewer understand immediately that this was rum, not vodka or any other clear liquor.

The name of the product (determined with the help of copywriter Jeff Mueller) came from the rum's recipe: it takes ten canes of sugar cane to produce one bottle of the product. It was a name that didn't feel fussy, a name the target buyer could say comfortably when ordering.

"Moët Hennessy is in Paris, and they really depended on us to reach the U.S. market correctly. The client wanted a name and design that clearly separated the product from vodka or any other clear liquor. We had to create a new language," recalls Werner. The new name not only refers to the main ingredient but also has the sense of an age-old recipe.

Werner and designer Sarah Nelson started their explorations of the bottle design by considering where it would live. To be successful in a club, a bottle must be bartender-friendly. Bartenders must be happy with how a bottle feels and performs. It can't slip out of their hands, and they want to look good while pouring from it. Plenty of testing occurred at this stage, all aimed at determining exact user preferences.

The cocktail buyer wants the bartender to look good, too. "For a $10 cocktail, it is as much about enjoying the mixing performance as it is about the taste of the finished drink," Werner notes.

With clearance from the client to design a custom bottle, Werner and Nelson considered carefully how its shape could become a vital part of the new identity. One design they particularly liked resembled an old flask with an offset neck, but the bottle manufacturer was unable to produce it in quantity.

Even though this shape felt good to the hand and the focus group liked it too, Werner says that in the end, she was glad the design didn't make it to the shelves. It was too trendy and therefore would not have had staying power.

"By the end of two years, everyone would have been tired of it. The bottle we decided on is simple and plain but appropriate and classic," she says.

The finished bottle has rounded shoulders and a long neck that is easy to hold, with little grippers. The base is of comfortable gripping width as well.

The bottle has aspects of modern and old, as does the product's logo. To design the mark, the designers studied heraldry as well as the history of Trinidad and the Caribbean, places that had a long history with rum. Sketching went on for several months as they mixed images of monkeys, sugarcane, currency—like seals, and many other engraved elements. They worked in a nondigital way, Werner recalls, drawing, redrawing, and combining tissues.

As they developed what is essentially a crest, flowing vegetation was added to suggest that the rum is a natural product. Crossed sugarcanes form an X to indicate the number of canes used for each bottle. A castle turret was inspired by the architecture of Trinidad and even France.

"The helmet? We don't really have a great reason for it. It just felt good. The important thing was to not get too highbrow with any one part," Werner says.

The final art, rendered by Elvis Swift, looks as though it may have been branded into wooden crates for hundreds of years. It is applied directly to the bottle. The contemporary touch comes from a warm, glossy orange paper label carrying the product name. The label is applied directly on top of the crest for a real contrast between old and new.

Werner says the design stands out in the club atmosphere, surrounded as it is with brands designed to be temporary. It is a classic look, meant to inspire the loyalty of drinkers who are comfortable with themselves. It is not intended to attract the trendy.

"The design catches customers' eyes, and the quality of the product sustains product loyalty," Werner says. The mix of contemporary design and traditional distilling is a strangely effective alchemy that is carried into the product's advertising. One ad shows a man in a tuxedo standing in a field of sugarcane—it's a strange but intriguing juxtaposition.

"It's a mix of old and new, of high and low. Together, the identity and the product look cool and right together," the designer says.

Here the designers screenprinted on both sides of the embossed bottle, creating many levels of interest. The type and crest are printed in two layers, orange directly under black. In this way, the orange shows through on one side, but the same image appears in black when the bottle is rotated.

(Above) More design trials combining paper labels, color, and printing.

(Left) As the new identity is played out in advertising and promotion, the same orange color and label are used—a clear identifier for the brand.

Cameo
Identity Design

Werner Design Werks, Minneapolis, Minnesota

Cameo is curious combination of beauty salon and social club. In fact, designer Sarah Nelson of Werner Design Werks calls it a "beauty lounge." Located near several trendy Minneapolis restaurants, Cameo is a place to see and be seen. The shop sells cosmetics and baubles, and it has a comfortable lounge area where the thirty- to forty-year-old set can gather to mingle, shop, get a manicure, and even enjoy a few drinks.

"The businesswomen who founded Cameo are sassy and smart," says Nelson. "They are very much people who would like to have their nails done and enjoy a martini at the same time. They offer lines of care products not available elsewhere. Their salon has definitely become a destination."

Nelson and partner Sharon Werner wanted to design a logo for Cameo that had the same sassy, irrepressible attitude as the establishment. The clients wanted something sexy and provocative but not sleazy—more like fan-dancing than striptease.

The designers came up with a number of directions that had appeal. The image of a powder puff had the right combination of beauty, attention to self, and pampering. (It actually ended up being used as a secondary application in the final identity; see secondary samples.) A Kewpie doll, frilly type, birds, butterflies, baby angels, and cupids were also considered.

But the idea the designers liked best showed the figure of a woman seated inside of an illuminated letter.

"The shape of the C suited the shape of the woman's back really well," says Nelson. The figure's hair flows around the letter almost like additional flourishes. Her black-clad legs kick out in a flirty way, and she winks playfully at the viewer. She is decidedly the prominent figure in the logo, but the letter still reads well.

To keep the woman somewhat chaste, Nelson had to do a lot of drawing and redrawing to expose just the right amount of breast. The emphasis had to be on beauty and sass, not overt sexiness.

The designers and the client were pleased with the finished logo. It's fun, yet definitely provocative. "Cameo is all about saying it is OK to look at yourself in the mirror and there's nothing wrong with playing with cosmetics. I think the logo expresses that," Nelson says.

Cameo

BEAUTY LOUNGE

Cameo

BEAUTY LOUNGE

Design Firm	Carbone Smolan
Client	Fortis
Project	Logo/Identity Design

The insurance market is a saturated one. Competitors and claims of all sorts of service abound. A risk-management company with a lesser-known name than Aetna or State Farm has to work hard to gain the customer's attention and explain what makes it special.

When Fortis, an international, integrated financial services provider, decided to offer its North American insurance operations as an initial public offering (IPO) on the New York Stock Exchange, the management team of the newly independent group had to create a whole new identity within months. The new company, named Assurant, required a system that would help its businesses—Assurant Solutions, Assurant Preneed, Assurant Health, and Assurant Employee Benefits—communicate their market focus and reinforce the coherence of the group. Finally, the identity had to say a lot about how Assurant's integrated offerings would benefit customers.

ASSURANT

Assurant's new logo and identity is bright, lively, and meaningful: It symbolizes the united energies of all lines of the company's subsidiaries.

> The challenge was to develop an identity that emphasized the coherence of the new group as well as its specialized niche services.

Landor Associates designed the original Fortis logo. Its design was meant to suggest the idea of Fortis being part of the communities where it had businesses. Carbone Smolan Agency, the design firm selected by Assurant to create the new identity, was asked to leverage the logo's bright, lively color system and visuals. The challenge was to develop an identity that emphasized the coherence of the new group as well as its specialized niche services.

FORTIS

The logo for Fortis, Assurant's previous identity, designed by Landor Associates, was meant to suggest that Fortis was an integral part of the communities in which it operates.

"Assurant integrates a trio of strengths: risk management expertise, administrative systems, and distribution relationships. It offers technical solutions to other companies and insurance to young people who are just coming off of their parents' insurance. It offers employee benefits to small- to mid-sized companies as well as preneed insurance—that is, insurance for funeral expenses," explains Catherine Goodman, Carbone Smolan project director. "We needed to somehow gather all of these strengths of the different businesses and communicate one strong company."

The Carbone Smolan team devised five distinct concepts for the client. The first had a connections focus. It demonstrated how the client connected with its customers, providing coverage for niche areas as well as

Carbone Smolan's woven graphic solution pulls together the core elements of the company. It can be displayed in a horizontal orientation with the wordmark, or the graphic can be run above the name (see introduction to article). The typeface Geometric was altered to mimic the rounded triangular shapes inside of the logo.

We needed to somehow gather all of these strengths of the different businesses and communicate one strong company.

excellent protection. This approach included graphics that showed bridges connecting land masses.

A second concept also looked at connections and bridges, but it was much more abstract. The designs in this group focused more on the wordmark.

One idea the designers liked was focusing graphically on the three capabilities the company offers. "We wanted to show that Assurant is specialized, focused, and integrated," says Dominick Ricci, Carbone Smolan designer for the project. This idea actually was the starting point for the final design solution, which came to be known as the "weave symbol."

> The idea was to show complex ideas such as aerodynamics through greatly simplified visual concepts.

To demonstrate the client's ability to handle complex concepts and situations clearly and competently, the design team also developed a tapestry concept. The weave in this design came from the letterforms themselves being woven together. "This showed that the company was complex. But the integration of the parts created a greater whole," explains Ricci.

The idea of growth emerged in the next set of designs. Here, the designers wanted to show Assurant's ability to form broad networks and achieve superior results for policyholders. These designs borrowed from images in nature to suggest growth.

Balance was the centerpiece of yet another set of designs. "The tightrope walkers were meant to show how Assurant brings balance to relationships," says Ricci. "The triangle forms a strong base that other things can rest safely on."

The penultimate design ended up the favorite. It demonstrated partnership. "These designs were all based around the ampersand," says Ricci.

But the idea that eventually emerged as the winner was a woven graphic that pulled together the core elements of the company. The final logo integrates the three niche offerings in a way that shows solid strength. A complete unit is formed, but the original three strengths are still distinct. Tucked inside is the suggestion of the letter A as well as a distinctly broad-based and stable triangle. (The idea for the A came from an Assurant executive with a keen interest in architecture.) To reinforce the shape, the designers modified the typeface Geometric for the wordmark to mimic the rounded triangle shape inside the mark.

"The typeface is very solid—it inspires confidence," says Ricci. "We ran it in a warm gray for even more strength and to play off the livelier colors we chose for the logo."

The other three colors—a blue, a green, and an orange—were favorites with the client almost from the beginning of the project. The traditional blue was Assurant's one remaining visual tie to the Fortis identity; the vibrant green and bright orange play well against it.

In advertising, the identity's vibrant color scheme is played out even further through metaphorical art—another way for the designers to explain in simple terms the client's complex product offerings.

The new color scheme became a crucial part of how the identity was introduced to the public. In ads that appeared in the *New York Times, Wall Street Journal,* and hundreds of other business and regional publications, the colors were played out through visual metaphors—a blue, green, and orange kite to demonstrate aerodynamics, and a similarly colored yo-yo to suggest gravity.

"The whole idea was to show complex ideas such as aerodynamics through greatly simplified visual concepts. The ads really stood out in the different publications," says Ricci. It is a value-added concept: Assurant specializes so it can make something as complicated as insurance simple for its customers.

Ricci and Goodman felt the final solution was fresh yet serious, appropriate for a company of Assurant's stature. "Boiling something as complex as a diversified insurance company down to something so simple and clear is very satisfying. There is a real story behind this logo; we really know what each stroke and color is about," Ricci says.

The new mark can be run in full color or no color, in large sizes or small, and still reads well.

The final logo integrates the three niche offerings in a way that shows solid strength.

Brooklyn Botanic Garden
Identity Design

Carbone Smolan, New York, New York

More than 100 years old in the making, Brooklyn Botanic Garden (BBG) was a living gem hidden just minutes from Manhattan. But beyond its immediate neighborhood, it was largely an unknown resource.

"People outside of the area did not realize what a great place it is," says Elizabeth Amorose, project director at Carbone Smolan Agency (CSA), the design firm that undertook a rebranding of the garden to correct this problem.

The garden's management is in the process of instituting plenty of facilities improvements, and it was clear a rebranding was necessary to raise the garden's status from a local attraction to a world-class institution. The Art Deco-like logo had been in use since the 1970s. The in-house team wanted something much more modern in feel.

"We did a lot of upfront strategizing with the client," says Carla Miller, design director at CSA. "We pared it down to several key words: *modern, growth,* and *plant life.* But no one wanted a literal drawing of a plant. They wanted a symbol."

After creating trial designs—including an abstract rendering of the Tree of Heaven (also known as the Chinese sumac); a tree described in the book *A Tree Grows in Brooklyn;* an abstract, rotating flower shape that evoked *change* and *beauty;* and an avant-garde monogram of BBG (eliminated because the garden couldn't go with a purely initial-based name)—CSA designers developed a mark that clearly demonstrated budding growth. Spare yet formal, the mark intertwines the three major focuses of

the garden: research and education (represented by blue), people and events (orange), and plant life (green).

"The mark represents plant life without being any particular plant," explains Amorose.

Another vital part of the identity is a long, arching line, actually one of the spires in the logo played out at a much greater scale. Based on the Fibonacci series, the equation that underlies the shape of all organic life, the blade is used as a container for imagery and text on the garden's website and across all of its materials—brochures, banners, and so on.

The complete identity is endlessly flexible. Interplayed with any number of floral and greenery elements from the garden, depending on the season and on events in the garden, it stays fresh and interesting.

Miller feels the mark and blade work well together to build a strong brand platform. "It's much more than just a logo. The new tagline, 'Where Plants Come to Life', which we also developed, is another important part," she explains.

Few large gardens do a good job of promoting themselves, so it was easy to make BBG stand out. "If the client wants to be known as a world-class facility, its identity cannot look homegrown," says Amorose. "BBG had the reputation of being more of a mom-and-pop operation. Now it is known as a world-class cultural institution."

Design Firm	Michael Osborne Design
Client	Target / Archer Farms
Project	Logo and Packaging Design

Target Corporation has become well known for offering its customers smart pricing and good design. Over the past decade, this value-added concept has been carried out across every category of product its stores carry.

At Target and Super Target stores, which include a full-service grocery, the company carries its own line of foods in addition to national brands. The Target brand, called Archer Farms, was meant to be an upscale line with a premium look. It sits on the shelves with a second Target brand that is the store's more price-conscious line. Archer Farms offerings were a bit more exotic; instead of just hot or mild salsa, for instance, it let the consumer choose between peach mango and three-bean varieties.

> The new logo and identity design had to look clearly more upscale than the price-conscious line.

The trouble was that a recent redesign of the price-conscious line made it look quite clean and attractive. In fact, it suddenly looked better than the Archer Farms brand. The upscale brand needed a new look, too. Target asked Michael Osborne Design, San Francisco—a design firm known for its classic but modern look—to undertake the identity makeover.

"Previously, the entire Archer Farms brand was color-coded in greens," explains principal Michael Osborne. "Whenever you saw the color green, you knew it was the private-label Target brand."

This simple approach was no longer effective. The new logo and identity design had to look clearly more upscale than the price-conscious line. It had to be consistently applicable to a wide variety of products, from popcorn to pasta and from bottled water to bottled sauces. Finally, it had to compete smartly with upscale national and regional brands.

These are relatively broad design directives, and the design team could have gone in many directions. Osborne's approach was to imagine the project objectives as a three-dimensional sphere. "When we are creating such a holistic system, we try to throw design darts and hit the sphere, but from all different directions, from different points of view. All the darts hit the target and accomplish the design goals, but in different ways," he explains.

His team presented a number of concepts. One direction featured round shapes and bright colors—"upscale, but more happy in a Target kind of

(Above) Archer Farms, Target Corporation's premium food line, now has a distinctive, upscale look, thanks to Michael Osborne Design.

(Right) When a more price-conscious Target food line was redesigned, the previous Archer Farms line, set entirely in green, no longer had the upscale look it needed to distinguish itself.

(Below) The Michael Osborne Design team explored a number of directions. These trials had a natural, earthy feel. They used kraft paper and unpretentious ties, combined with simple typography and colors, to create an Old-World-meets-modern-Target look.

(Above) These explorations were more in keeping with the storewide Target identity: bouncy, geometric, bright. Colors and typography were also vibrant and modern.

It is just as important to cover the full array of ideas, even the extreme ones, so the client is exposed to the full range of creative possibilities.

The reason the design is successful is because it is so different from the standard Target branding and the red bull's-eye.

way," explains Osborne. Highly geometric, this design approach complemented the Target logo with its primary color palette and shapes.

Another suggested design direction had a natural, earthy feeling. It used natural kraft paper and bags for packaging, interesting and unusual structures and closures, and the branding and typography had an Old-World-Italy-meets-modern-Target look.

A third concept looked simply gorgeous and gourmet, says Osborne, like the packaging that might be found on a line of foods in a specialty market. It featured luscious photography, a rich color palette, and elegant typography. It was perhaps too upscale, he adds, but it is just as important to cover the full array of ideas—even the extreme ones—so the client is exposed to the full range of creative possibilities.

Osborne stands behind all directions that are presented in these types of projects. He often makes recommendations based on what his team feels will compete most effectively in the marketplace. In this case, Target agreed that a "French country-with-a-modern-twist" concept worked best. At its center was a simple brand identity: a rooster, sitting proudly inside a low-slung oval, together with the motto "Tasty Food, Tasty Price." This mark sat easily on all types of packaging: bags, cans, bottle, jars. Combined with a palette of rich reds, greens, blues, yellows, and black, the logo stands out as a ready identifier on shelves populated with obnoxiously colored packaging.

Aesthetics aside, the identity worked well for every sort of printing the Archer Farms packaging required. Its simplicity allowed it to be stamped onto plastic bags as successfully and cleanly as it could be four-color offset-printed on paper.

Some products utilized beautiful, up-close color photographs set off by a dark hunter-green background with a diamond pattern. Other products featured clear structures or unusual substrates, such as a metallic silver-foil coffee bag.

Osborne feels one reason the design is successful is because it is so different from the standard Target branding and the red bull's-eye, yet it works well in context and complements the other offerings to the Target consumer.

"It's an upscale food line. When you pick up a product, it really does look delicious, while being reasonably priced," he says. "'Expect more, pay less', the Target motto, has never been truer."

(Above) The final identity looks decidedly gourmet. It has a rich color scheme, upscale typography, and a sense of history.

(Opposite) Applied to packaging, the new logo and identity cuts through the jumble of color and graphics on the Target shelves. It is so simple that it prints well on any substrate and through any printing method.

Hearts in San Francisco
Identity Design

Michael Osborne Design, San Francisco, California

Hearts in San Francisco was an initiative by private citizens to raise money for the San Francisco General Hospital Foundation. It was modeled on efforts made in other cities across the country in which a geographically apt icon is dressed by many local artists. In Chicago, cows were appropriate. In San Francisco, it had to be hearts.

Michael Osborne Design was asked by the Hearts steering committee to create the two crucial portions of the effort's identity: First, he designed a pair of large, three-dimensional hearts. Artists could pick one of the two to paint or otherwise alter to express their message. Once all 130 sculptures were done, they were displayed throughout the city as public art installations. These formed the public face of the program.

The two hearts had different personalities. "The first thing I thought of was a big, round, full heart with its point on the ground—a big, voluptuous heart. I wanted a different form for the second one. I actually based it on a sculpture I did in seventh-grade shop class. It has big, intersecting plates," the designer says.

Osborne also created a logo for the program, to be used on collateral, the group's website (www.heartsinsf.com), advertising, and on banners and other signage. It was important that the logo not compete with the artists' sculptures for attention. The design had to be in line with traditional corporate identity, yet be more expressive.

His solution, created after about 100 trials with a paintbrush (all untouched by Photoshop, he says), is clearly related to the arts, but its solid typography grounds it in a formal way. "It needed flair, spontaneity, and energy, but it does not compete with the artists," Osborne says.

At the end of the exhibition, a live auction was held to sell the twenty-five hearts that had special meaning to the city or were created by the most prominent artists. The remainder were auctioned off on eBay. The proceeds, combined with the sales of a keepsake book that displayed all of the hearts, raised just over $2 million for the Foundation.

Osborne says that although the project was meant to be a one-time event, the organizers have received many requests to do it again.

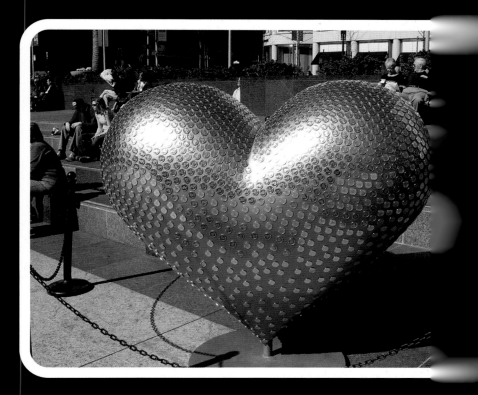

collections and sketches

	A	**B**	**C**	**D**

1

LOGO SEARCH

Keywords: Initials

Type: ○ Symbol ○ Typographic ○ Combo ● All

2

AFTER 5
COMPANIES

A E T H E R

3

AIRLUME
CANDLES

ALLSCRIPTS

4

AGENDAONE

AIAS

5

A TO Z MEDIA

ⓓ = Design Firm   ⓒ = Client

	A	B	C	D	
1					1
2					2
3					3
4					4
5					5

Ⓓ = Design Firm   Ⓒ = Client

1A Ⓓ Paul Black Design Ⓒ Burns Service Company   1B Ⓓ Henjum Creative Ⓒ Badger Paper Mills   1C Ⓓ Ikola designs... Ⓒ Brunswick United Methodist Church   1D Ⓓ Landkamer Partners, Inc. Ⓒ Biogenics

2A Ⓓ Steven O'Connor Ⓒ B 10   2B Ⓓ Ross Hogin Design Ⓒ Boticelli Pastaworks   2C Ⓓ Ikola designs... Ⓒ burningham Weavers   2D Ⓓ Mindgruve Ⓒ Blue Motif

3A Ⓓ Whaley Design, Ltd Ⓒ Chargo Printing, Inc.   3B Ⓓ MINE Ⓒ Blaney Kravitz/Comira   3C Ⓓ GRAF d'SIGN creative boutique Ⓒ Cybico   3D Ⓓ Mariqua Design Ⓒ Clone

4A Ⓓ AKOFA Creative Ⓒ Self Promotional   4B Ⓓ Werner Design Werks Ⓒ Chandler Atwood   4C Ⓓ R&D Thinktank Ⓒ Capital Plan   4D Ⓓ Gardner Design Ⓒ Corry Dance Academy

5A Ⓓ Jonathan Rice & Company Ⓒ Champion Energy   5B Ⓓ angryporcupine*design Ⓒ Cheryl Dailey   5C Ⓓ Werner Design Werks Ⓒ College of Visual Arts   5D Ⓓ Duffy & Partners Ⓒ Duffy & Partners

A	B	C	D

A **B** **C** **D**

1

2

3

4

5

  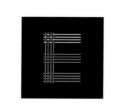 

	A	B	C	D	
1	 EFFICIENTPRODUCTS	 ENGENIUM	 Emerald Graphics		1
2		E24 INTERNETACTIVE		 FILIGREE	2
3		 FOLINGER	FascinA	FAR FETCHED SPIRITS	3
4	 FRANKLYN MEDIA GROUP	 EYEWEAR GALLERY		 comgroup	4
5			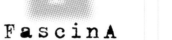 G.W.Engineering	 HORYZON GRUPA WYDAWNICZA	5

Ⓓ = Design Firm   Ⓒ = Client

1A Ⓓ Dotzero Design Ⓒ Ecos 1B Ⓓ Peterson & Company Ⓒ Engenium 1C Ⓓ Brand Bird Ⓒ emerald Graphics 1D Ⓓ FutureBrand Ⓒ Millicom Argentina

2A Ⓓ ODM oficina de diseño y marketing Ⓒ Eléctrica Bahia 2B Ⓓ Diagram Ⓒ E24 Internet Club 2C Ⓓ marc usa Ⓒ Fleck Photography 2D Ⓓ Duffy & Partners Ⓒ Thymes

3A Ⓓ McMillian Design Ⓒ Fulton Street BID 3B Ⓓ Mode Design Studio Ⓒ Folinger Mountainwear 3C Ⓓ designlab, inc Ⓒ Weissman's Dance 3D Ⓓ IMAGEHAUS Ⓒ Far Fetched Spirits

4A Ⓓ Interrobang Design Collaborative, Inc. Ⓒ FM Group Public Relations 4B Ⓓ Tactical Magic Ⓒ The Eyewear Gallery 4C Ⓓ Allen Creative Ⓒ Grace Fellowship 4D Ⓓ ComGroup Ⓒ ComGroup

5A Ⓓ Diagram Ⓒ Kulczyk Foundation 5B Ⓓ GetElevatedDesign.com Ⓒ Green Lotus Grounds 5C Ⓓ Crackerbox Ⓒ G.W.Engineering 5D Ⓓ Diagram Ⓒ Horyzon Publishing

	A	B	C	D
1				
2				
3				
4				
5				

ⅅ = Design Firm ⅭⅭ = Client

1A ⅅ Diagram Ⅽ Horse Publishing   1B ⅅ Gardner Design Ⅽ Hustler   1C ⅅ Ross Hogin Design Ⅽ HRCentral   1D ⅅ Deep Design Ⅽ The Henritze Company, LLC

2A ⅅ Zed+Zed+Eye Creative Communications Ⅽ Hilliards Insulation   2B ⅅ Dialekt Design Ⅽ Timex (JDK)   2C ⅅ Gardner Design Ⅽ Hustler   2D ⅅ Sibley Peteet Ⅽ Horizon Printing

3A ⅅ Sibley Peteet Ⅽ Ryan and Dinah Street   3B ⅅ Q Ⅽ Hessen Chemie   3C ⅅ Ikola designs... Ⅽ Ikola designs...   3D ⅅ Ardoise Design Ⅽ Immotik inc.

4A ⅅ Bryan Cooper Design Ⅽ Impact Productions   4B ⅅ Sockeye Creative Ⅽ ieLogic   4C ⅅ Eisenberg and Associates Ⅽ IT Rescue   4D ⅅ Kendall Creative Shop, Inc. Ⅽ Jarvis Press

5A ⅅ B.L.A. Design Company Ⅽ Nathan Good   5B ⅅ DDB Dallas Ⅽ Kemp Academy of Tae Kwon Do and Hapkido   5C ⅅ Lesniewicz Associates Ⅽ Kuhlman Corp.   5D ⅅ Funk/Levis & Associates, Inc. Ⅽ Kelly King & Associates

	A	B	C	D
1	**kea** Quality Print		 KONTRAPUNKT	 PREMIUM LUSOMUNDO
2	 Landes Investments	 lenox graphics		 MERCURY
3	 mobimax		 Metro	
4			MUTTMINSTER  THE IOWA MUTT SHOW ANIMAL RESCUE LEAGUE OF IOWA	McM1LLEN
5	 **MicroInteractive**	 merchant**logix**		 MetroNational BANK & TRUST

 ▶ = Design Firm ⦿ = Client

1A ▶ Diagram ⦿ KEA 1B ▶ www.iseedots.com ⦿ Kress Design 1C ▶ Delikatessen ⦿ Kontrapunkt 1D ▶ Brandia ⦿ Lusomundo

2A ▶ Richards Brock Miller Mitchell & Associates ⦿ Landes Investments 2B ▶ Lenox Graphics ⦿ Lenox Graphics 2C ▶ Thomas Manss & Company ⦿ Metamorphosis 2D ▶ Pixelspace ⦿ The Jackson Group

3A ▶ Grapefruit ⦿ Mobimax 3B ▶ Idle hands Design ⦿ M Digital 3C ▶ FutureBrand ⦿ E.Wong-Peru 3D ▶ thomas-vasquez.com ⦿ universal music/motown records

4A ▶ Hubbell Design Works ⦿ Mavericks Custom Trousers 4B ▶ 68Design ⦿ Mouton Salon 4C ▶ The Meyocks Group ⦿ Animal Rescue League of Iowa 4D ▶ CAPSULE ⦿ Paladin

5A ▶ Misenheimer Creative, Inc/misenheimer.com ⦿ microinteractive/network 21 5B ▶ rajasandhu.com ⦿ MerchantLogix 5C ▶ Simon & Goetz Design ⦿ Maeser 5D ▶ judson design associates ⦿ MetroNational

	A	B	C	D
1	 MetroWest		 NUANCE	
2		 Netscape®	 napa valley vintners	 Notiva
3	 NouvelleVie Opaque	 NUANCE AV	 orthomol	 oretum
4	 THE OCEAN CLUB		 OTTER CREEK MALL	
5	 PIVOT180™			

A   B   C   D

      1

      2

      3

      4

5

Ⓓ = Design Firm   Ⓒ = Client

1A Ⓓ R&D Thinktank Ⓒ Quady Painting 1B Ⓓ KOESTER design Ⓒ Q ink 1C Ⓓ ROAD design inc. Ⓒ Pairgain 1D Ⓓ Fernandez Design Ⓒ TorchQuest

2A Ⓓ Jon Flaming Design Ⓒ Proposed Quark Logo 2B Ⓓ UlrichPinciotti Design Group Ⓒ Quantum Group 2C Ⓓ Wilkinson Media Ⓒ I-Quotient 2D Ⓓ Axiom Design Partners Ⓒ Quality Press

3A Ⓓ Allen Creative Ⓒ River Rehab 3B Ⓓ octane inc. Ⓒ Rustad Marketing 3C Ⓓ Edward Allen Ⓒ Revolve Motion 3D Ⓓ Gardner Design Ⓒ Relianz Bank

4A Ⓓ The Meyocks Group Ⓒ rubberdisc.com 4B Ⓓ rajasandhu.com Ⓒ First Rate 4C Ⓓ Rick Johnson & Company Ⓒ Rick Johnson & Company 4D Ⓓ Gardner Design Ⓒ Russell Public Relations

5A Ⓓ Gardner Design Ⓒ Relianz Bank 5B Ⓓ Henjum Creative Ⓒ Oshkosh Symphony Orchestra 5C Ⓓ Moscato Design Ⓒ Simpson's 5D Ⓓ Strategy Studio Ⓒ Strategy Studio

77

	A	B	C	D
1				
2				
3				
4				
5				

A B C D

1

2

3

4

5

Ⓓ = Design Firm   Ⓒ = Client

1A Ⓓ Launchpad Creative Ⓒ Launchpad Creative   1B Ⓓ Kendall Creative Shop, Inc. Ⓒ WestFork Pipeline   1C Ⓓ Gabriel Kalach*VISUAL communication Ⓒ W2 Media   1D Ⓓ Bryan Cooper Design Ⓒ Wood Window Store

2A Ⓓ Jon Flaming Design Ⓒ Watermark Community Church   2B Ⓓ joe miller's company Ⓒ Willow Technology   2C Ⓓ proteus Ⓒ Wellington   2D Ⓓ fallindesign studio Ⓒ Wood Stock Exchange

3A Ⓓ Exti Dzyn Ⓒ Wolfgang Puck   3B Ⓓ maximo, inc. Ⓒ Brooktree Corporation   3C Ⓓ The Joe Bosack Graphic Design Co. Ⓒ AND 1   3D Ⓓ Brandia Ⓒ Audaxys

4A Ⓓ Brandia Ⓒ Yorn   4B Ⓓ Zapata Design Ⓒ Zapata Design   4C Ⓓ The Meyocks Group Ⓒ i wireless   4D Ⓓ Werner Design Werks Ⓒ VH1

5A Ⓓ ArtGraphics, ru Ⓒ 1 September Publishing House   5B Ⓓ Strategy Studio Ⓒ First Timers   5C Ⓓ 2cdesign Ⓒ Two by Two for AIDS and Art   5D Ⓓ Hubbell Design Works Ⓒ Centex Homes

	A	B	C	D
1				
2				
3				
4				
5				ReUnion 2001

ⓓ = Design Firm   ⓒ = Client

1A ⓓ Deep Design ⓒ i3Media 1B ⓓ Owen Design ⓒ DSM Art Center 1C ⓓ UNO ⓒ Minneapolis 1D ⓓ Direct Design Visual Branding ⓒ fifth avenue

2A ⓓ mattisimo ⓒ Six Stich 2B ⓓ Chimera Design ⓒ Tabcorp 2C ⓓ Day six Creative ⓒ Day Six Creative 2D ⓓ oakley design studios ⓒ Kink fm 102

3A ⓓ Methodologie ⓒ RC Hedreen 3B ⓓ GSD&M ⓒ GSD&M 3C ⓓ Mindspike Design, LLC ⓒ Eighth Floor Recording 3D ⓓ Eleven Feet Media ⓒ Eleven Feet Media

4A ⓓ Miles Design ⓒ Urban Forward 4B ⓓ judson design associates ⓒ Unused 4C ⓓ Shawn Hazen Graphic Design ⓒ 41Seventy Studio 4D ⓓ Shift design ⓒ BP

5A ⓓ Edward Allen ⓒ 665 Almost Evil 5B ⓓ Turney Creative ⓒ Momentum Ministries 5C ⓓ DDB ⓒ 1508 inc. 5D ⓓ Aurora Design ⓒ Union College Magazine

M5 Coke
Identity Design

mk12, Kansas City, Missouri

How do you turn a consumer product into an event? That's what the Coca-Cola Company asked the design office mk12, as well as four other offices around the world. The answer: Take two of the most common design icons found anywhere—the Coke logo and the Coke bottle—and transform them into something that defies expectations.

A core creative team at Coke contacted five teams known for their thought-provoking graphics and motion graphics work: mk12 (Kansas City, MO/North America); REX and Tennant McKay (South Africa); Lobo (Brazil); The Designers Republic (United Kingdom); and Caviar (Japan). The client's instructions were minimal: Each team should create a new Coke identity using a metal bottle and building off of the word *optimism.* Each team was also asked to produce a music video bringing its design to life through motion and sound.

Ben Radatz, partner at mk12, explains that Coke is not trying to build its brand through the project. In fact, the five designs will be distributed only to a select group of clubs frequented by people in tune with the arts.

"Coke is more than a brand—the words *soft drink* and *Coke* are almost synonymous. Traditional branding through advertising doesn't hurt anything, but it really doesn't help the company much anymore. Everyone knows what the bottle and logo look like already," Radatz says. "With this project, Coke wants to promote the arts, in an altruistic way, as it did before with Keith Haring and Andy Warhol. The company is helping people reconsider everything."

For their design, Radatz says his team wanted to build on the way that the product's logo complements the bottle shape. The result was a complicated series of swirls, graphic flowers, silhouetted shapes, and flat colors that wrap the entire aluminum bottle and are completely unlike traditional Coke graphics. Every element can be easily animated.

Each design also has a hidden element: when placed under black light, such as might be used in a club, a hidden, secondary design is revealed. This multilevel scheme adds to the exploration and discovery aspects of what Coke calls the M5 project.

"The designs blow people's minds. They are used to a certain type of branding, and this is a complete 180 for them," Radatz says. "Converse and Volkswagen have also done experimental design like this. It could be an interesting trend in corporate design."

It was fascinating at the project's end, he adds, to discover that all the firms took the same approach—building on the swirl—as mk12, although none had consulted with the others. It's a revealing insight into the power of the Coke logo worldwide.

See all five bottle designs at www.them5.com, including the music video mk12 produced with the group Guided by Voices.

	A	B	C	D

1

LOGO SEARCH

Keywords **Typography**

Type: ○ Symbol ○ Typographic ○ Combo ● All

blo

(poetry center san josé)

2

s☺ript:

ink

edge

Third point

3

w!se
working in support of education

karen hill scott

entertrainingEtc
educational technologies and consulting

.planum:

4

oyuna

Explore

Velotools

tilfréttir

5

seas

ourture CARE

OBSERVA

JASON
AND THE ARGONAUTS

D = Design Firm   **C** = Client

1A **D** Jejak, rumah iklan dan disain **C** Zone   1B **D** Rotor Design **C** Rotor Design   1C **D** dandy idea **C** Texas Commission on the Arts   1D **D** Future Brand **C** Wines of Chile

2A **D** Bakken Creative Co. **C** Frascati Restaurant   2B **D** GSCS **C** Bridge Business partners   2C **D** Orange Creative **C** Morgan Hair   2D **D** Werner Design Werks **C** Indochine

3A **D** dedstudios **C** Wildflower Linen   3B **D** Times Infinity **C** Home & Habitat   3C **D** Judson design associates **C** Lumina   3D **D** NeoGine Communication Design Ltd **C** Stephanie Pietkiewicz

4A **D** Tiffany Design **C** Classico Wine   4B **D** The Design Poole **C** The Military Shop   4C **D** Brand Navigation **C** Island Lodge   4D **D** Felixsockwell.com **C** nyc2012

5A **D** Fredrik Lewander **C** Dobb Production   5B **D** dialect Design **C** Toboggan Design   5C **D** jsDesignCo. **C** Throttle, LTD.   5D **D** CAPSULE **C** Lumens

83

	A	B	C	D
1	**Da:Da:Da.**	white *coloured by you*	clearw're	 spa orange
2	the great lakes center for **autism**	Warm Springs REHABILITATION SYSTEM	H!gh F!ve	brilliant corporation
3	g⊙⊙dies	cork screw	9below	mark. garrison
4	cutcost.com	Institute for Emerging Issues	twistology	bepositive 
5	stepxstep	micropelt	loglogic	(>erb)

D = Design Firm   **C** = Client

1A **D** ZEBRA design branding **C** Da Da Da 1B **D** Brandia **C** White 1C **D** Hornall Anderson **C** Clearwire 1D **D** Hirshorn Zuckerman Design Group **C** Spa Orange

2A **D** UlrichPinciotti Design Group **C** Great Lakes Center for Autism 2B **D** Roger Christian & Co **C** Warm Springs Rehabilitation System 2C **D** Peters Design **C** High Five 2D **D** logobyte **C** Brilliant Health Corporation

3A **D** Stand Advertising **C** Rich Products 3B **D** A3 Design **C** Corkscrew Wine Bar 3C **D** Brainding **C** 9 Below 3D **D** Vigor Graphic Design, LLC. **C** Mark Garrison Salon

4A **D** Thomas Manss & Company **C** Cutcost.com 4B **D** Polemic Design **C** Ralph Appelbaum Associates 4C **D** Lisa Speer **C** Twistology 4D **D** Brandia **C** Galp Energia

5A **D** Lesniewicz Associates **C** Step-by-Step 5B **D** Thomas Manss & Company **C** Infineon 5C **D** Stiles+co **C** LogLogic 5D **D** Eric Baker Design Assoc. Inc **C** verb Interactive

	A	B	C	D

 pharmaco Genomics

 astra lodge ❄

Biokorntakt

JanTzen

1

barcode

 mad river post

 powersquid

tiGo

2

 fuse

ecoffice

n·able

 redfish

3

HUMAN RIGHTS CANADIAN MUSEUM FOR

AMNES'A
LEST WE FORGET

 TWIST

CHANGE OF SPACE

4

 CREACTIVO

ARSENIGO

NOTORIOUS

PIVOTAL
FITNESS

5

Ⓓ = Design Firm   Ⓒ = Client

1A Ⓓ Bristol-Myers Squibb Ⓒ Bristol-Myers Squibb 1B Ⓓ Chimera Design Ⓒ Astra Lodge 1C Ⓓ Off-Leash Studios Ⓒ Luke O'Malley/Biokorntakt 1D Ⓓ Sandstrom Design Ⓒ Jantzen

2A Ⓓ Bakken Creative Co. Ⓒ Stark Properties 2B Ⓓ sheean design Ⓒ Urban Design 2C Ⓓ label brand Ⓒ Trident Design, LLC. 2D Ⓓ FutureBrand Ⓒ Millicom

3A Ⓓ Liska + Associates Communication Design Ⓒ Fuse 3B Ⓓ Corporate Express Ⓒ Corporate Express 3C Ⓓ Harwood Kirsten Leigh Mc Coy Ⓒ EDS solutions enterprise 3D Ⓓ Off-Leash Studios Ⓒ razorfish, inc.

4A Ⓓ Polemic Design Ⓒ Michael Reiter 4B Ⓓ Lars Lawson Ⓒ The Damien Center 4C Ⓓ mccoycreative Ⓒ Twist Soda 4D Ⓓ Cisneros Design Ⓒ Change of Space

5A Ⓓ brainding Ⓒ Creactivo 5B Ⓓ ODM oficina de diseño y marketing Ⓒ Arsenio 5C Ⓓ ZONA Design, Inc Ⓒ The Biography Chanel 5D Ⓓ greteman group Ⓒ pivotal fitness

	A	**B**	**C**	**D**
1	EROICA	MIYAKE	SEE-USA	FIVEPOINT
2	LUCINA	SKWISH fun classic	BONEY'S BAYSIDE MARKET	WORLD UNCORKED
3	©h®is™as	MARIXA	RIVALS	SBANE
4	MIKEY	It's happening in ALASKA	PUSH	BENT
5	SRTECE FTFSU NORTON TFSUF SECRET STUFF ERSCET FUFTS TERECS UFTSF	NEW YORK PUBLIC LIBRARY DONNELL BRANCH	HŌM	CODA

B
Identity Design

Miles Newlyn, London, United Kingdom

Miles Newlyn's logo design is as different from the mainstream as it could possibly be. It challenges clients and designers alike. That's because of the unique angle from which he views the field. He cites a quote from Jung in *Man and His Symbols:*

"A word or image is symbolic when it implies something more than its obvious and immediate meaning. It has a wider 'unconscious' aspect that is never precisely defined or explained . . . . As the mind explores the symbol, it is led to ideas that lie beyond the grasp of reason."

The quote explains a lot to the London-based Newlyn. "What I find great about the quote is that you can forget any definition of what a logo is and consider anything as a logo, if it is saying what you want it to. In the context of branding, for example, an auto manufacturer's cars *are* its primary symbol. The cars are the corporate communication. This is the reason why auto manufacturers have adopted almost photographic rendering of their badges/mascots for their logos," Newlyn says. Logos don't appear in viewers' minds as flat things, rather just as things.

To create a logo for B, a prospective brand for a mobile communications business in the Seychelles, the designer had this in mind. After researching the Seychelles, a scattering of lush tropical islands in the Indian Ocean, Newlyn became interested in the coco de mer, an ancient palm tree unique to the islands. The trees produce the so-called love nut, a symbol so important that it is featured on the local currency. The shape was an appropriate and evocative connection to the islands.

"What might a service company's rendering of its imaginary mascot look like? Also, companies increasingly see themselves as a destination: not what you are buying, but where it takes you," the designer says.

Working with long-time collaborator Ali Coleman, Newlyn crafted a form that is many things: the letterform *B,* a suggestion of the form of the coco de mer nut, and all sorts of sexually provocative shapes. The form is decidedly three-dimensional and full of energy, representing the company's locus as communications provider within this small community.

In designing a new logo, it's crucial not only to represent the client but also to understand the client's audience. "Much of what I do is typographic, so it's important to understand how various people feel about letter styles. Different audiences see different things. These nuances are often a source of inspiration to either build upon or react against. A business for which I'm creating a logo may want to be considered a part of a nation, or it may not," Newlyn says. "B decidedly needed to be connected to its home.

"The solution gained the client's confidence in our understanding their audience, and it also opened their eyes to a creative experience. In this sense, the logo was accepted. Clients often take the rare opportunity of their branding project as an enjoyable experience with the creative industry, and not all branding projects have to end with a protectable asset," says Newlyn. "I like this way of working, and if the client decides to implement strategies and visuals I've worked on, that's a bonus."

A	B	C	D

1

LOGO SEARCH

Keywords [Enclosures]

Type: ○ Symbol ○ Typographic ○ Combo ● All

    GEAR UP

 HERO PATTERN

2

 DELL

 thirst.

 beeline

 HOME THYMES

3

 PIXIE MATÉ

 100 YEARS 100 RANCHERS

 THE BOTTLE SHOP

 WOW BAKING COMPANY

4

 tangerine

 Simon

 TALK ON

 Chuy's fine TEX MEX

5

 OLIVE LEAF

 LEMON FRESH KIDS

 cake

 Muscletones

---

Ⓓ = Design Firm　Ⓒ = Client

1C Ⓓ Coleman Creative Ⓒ Gunn Automotive　1D Ⓓ Alphabet Arm Design Ⓒ Kristin Bredimus/Hero Pattern

2A Ⓓ DDB Ⓒ Dell　2B Ⓓ Nita B. Creative Ⓒ thirst　2C Ⓓ Kym Abrams Design Ⓒ North Lawndale Employment Network　2D Ⓓ Duffy & Partners Ⓒ Thymes

3A Ⓓ Brand Engine Ⓒ Pixie Maté　3B Ⓓ Campbell Fisher Design Scott Baxter　3C Ⓓ Todd M. LeMieux Design Ⓒ The Bottle Shop　3D Ⓓ Mary Hutchinson Design LLC Ⓒ WOW Baking Company

4A Ⓓ Kaimere Ⓒ Fairmont Hotels　4B Ⓓ KOESTER design Ⓒ Span International　4C Ⓓ Design and Image Ⓒ TalkOn　4D Ⓓ GSD&M Ⓒ Chuy's Tex-Mex

5A Ⓓ Duffy & Partners Ⓒ Thymes　5B Ⓓ Alphabet Arm Design Ⓒ Tim McCoy　5C Ⓓ sheean design Ⓒ Cake Productions　5D Ⓓ David Kampa Ⓒ Muscletones Sport Wraps

88

	A	B	C	D	
1					1
2					2
3					3
4					4
5					5

ⓓ = Design Firm   **ⓒ** = Client

1A ⓓ Modern Dog Design Co. ⓒ Brown Paper Tickets   1B ⓓ SKOOTA ⓒ Whiteleaf (proposed)   1C ⓓ Peterson & Company ⓒ University of Texas at Dallas School of Management   1D ⓓ Kern Design Group ⓒ North Castle Partners

2A ⓓ NeoGine Communication Design Ltd ⓒ City Print Communication   2B ⓓ Parachute Design ⓒ IVY Hotel + Residence   2C ⓓ GSD&M ⓒ Austin Museum of Art   2D ⓓ Landkamer Partners, Inc. ⓒ Epigram

3A ⓓ Edward Allen ⓒ La Zona Rosa   3B ⓓ www.iseedots.com ⓒ The Castle Group   3C ⓓ FutureBrand ⓒ Avianca Colombia   3D ⓓ Duffy & Partners ⓒ Thymes

4A ⓓ Visual Inventor Ltd. Co. ⓒ Digimedia   4B ⓓ Sandstrom Design ⓒ Fuse   4C ⓓ Pix Design, inc. ⓒ Union Market   4D ⓓ LogoDesignSource.com ⓒ INKI

5A ⓓ judson design associates ⓒ Story Films   5B ⓓ Dr. Alderete ⓒ Spatium magazine   5C ⓓ strategyone ⓒ Airgate International   5D ⓓ Mirko Ilic Corp ⓒ Spread, Inc

	A	B	C	D
1				
2			(AXXIOM)	
3				
4				
5			(mr. Kabob)	

Ⓓ = Design Firm   Ⓒ = Client

1A Ⓓ Lunar Design Ⓒ Spider   1B Ⓓ dale harris Ⓒ forbean   1C Ⓓ Sharp Communications, Inc. Ⓒ Pier Sixty The Lighthouse   1D Ⓓ NeoGine Communication Design Ltd Ⓒ Schoc Chocolatier

2A Ⓓ Tunglid Advertising Agency ehg. Ⓒ KB LÍF   2B Ⓓ Felixsockwell.com Ⓒ felix sockwell   2C Ⓓ SKOOTA Ⓒ Consolidated Shoes   2D Ⓓ Turner Duckworth Ⓒ Refreshment Brands

3A Ⓓ Dotzero Design Ⓒ Portland Metro   3B Ⓓ Church Logo Gallery Ⓒ Church Logo Gallery   3C Ⓓ element Ⓒ element   3D Ⓓ Strategy Studio Ⓒ Bruce Coleman Photo Library

4A Ⓓ Design and Image Ⓒ Joe Hancock   4B Ⓓ Brand Engine Ⓒ inhaus   4C Ⓓ FWIS Ⓒ Readymech   4D Ⓓ Gabriel Kalach * V I S U A L communication Ⓒ Script & Scribble

5A Ⓓ SD Graphic Design Ⓒ Crabtree Lane Studio   5B Ⓓ Bryan Cooper Design Ⓒ Mod Fifties Modern   5C Ⓓ Floor 84 Studio Ⓒ Mr. Kabob   5D Ⓓ morrow mckenzie design Ⓒ New York Tix

A	**B**	**C**	**D**	
				1
				2
				3
				4
				5

D = Design Firm **C** = Client

1A **D** Living Creative Design **C** WOWOW Entertainments Inc. 1B **D** Ammunition **C** Joe Public Relations Ltd 1C **D** The Collaboration **C** The Collaboration 1D **D** Living Creative Design **C** Korea IT Network

2A **D** sheean design **C** Pyramid Creative Studios 2B **D** Alphabet Arm Design **C** Eric Klein 2C **D** Parachute Design **C** RMF Group 2D **D** David Kampa **C** Penny's Pastries

3A **D** morrow mckenzie design **C** Carafe 3B **D** Fauxkoi **C** Lily Red 3C **D** Lars Lawson **C** The Damien Center 3D **D** The Flores Shop **C** Gridlock Paintball Team

4A **D** Idea Girl Design **C** Nasty's 4B **D** R&R Partners **C** Atomic Testing Museum 4C **D** greteman group **C** cosmic cocktails 4D **D** Werner Design Werks **C** Style Stretch

5A **D** Dan Rood Design **C** John Hutton 5B **D** Stephan and Herr **C** Fleer 5C **D** UNO **C** Target Stores 5D **D** Shift design **C** PTM

LOGO SEARCH

Keywords **Display Type**

Type: ◯ Symbol ◯ Typographic ◯ Combo ◉ All

	A	B	C	D
1				
2				
3				
4				
5				

ⓓ = Design Firm   ⓒ = Client

1A ⓓ Gardner Design ⓒ Epic   1B ⓓ Zipper Design ⓒ Nicola Vruwink   1C ⓓ dale harris ⓒ the remedy festival   1D ⓓ Thielen Designs ⓒ Hyperactive Music Magazine

2A ⓓ Studio Stubborn Sideburn ⓒ Stubborn Sideburn   2B ⓓ Blacktop Creative ⓒ Kansas City   2C ⓓ David Kampa ⓒ Live Oak Brewing Company   2D ⓓ Delikatessen ⓒ Stefan Engel Inc.

3A ⓓ SKOOTA ⓒ Serious Robots   3B ⓓ Zona Design, Inc ⓒ Lenny Kravitz   3C ⓓ switchfoot creative ⓒ Fusco Leathrworks   3D ⓓ element ⓒ element alternate logo

4A ⓓ Zed+Zed+Eye Creative Communications ⓒ Rondo's Restaurant   4B ⓓ M3 Advertising Design ⓒ navegante group   4C ⓓ oakley design studios ⓒ gunther   4D ⓓ Sam's Garage ⓒ Sam's Garage

5A ⓓ M3 Advertising Design ⓒ Sonny Ahuja   5B ⓓ Ammunition ⓒ The Rights Company Ltd   5C ⓓ The Flores Shop ⓒ Agony Press Publishing   5D ⓓ nicelogo.com ⓒ Century City Jazz Festival

93

	A	B	C	D
1	MACA 76		darkwood dub	kidWise
2	dub	CTN SOLUTIONS	bits	
3	GRATAROLA JAMÁS! HISTORIETAS	CHANGO MACHO	visionworks	TAP TAP PORTUGAL
4	THE ★★★ NATIONAL PASTIME	LONG JOHN SILVER'S	CATCH DESIGN STUDIO	xodus ministries
5		ART 316		

	A	B	C	D

    1

    2

    3

 4

  5

R&D Thinktank
Identity Design

Tom Nynas, Dallas, Texas

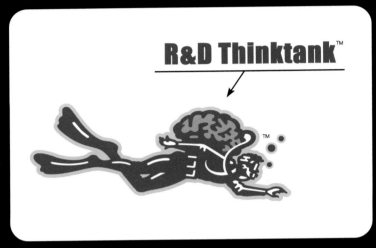

R&D Thinktank is a young ad agency, located in Dallas, founded in 2001 by Doug Rucker and Jan Deatherage, both veterans of The Richards Group. Their goal was to create a company where clients could acquire full-service capabilities to build their brands, but with a high level of senior involvement that larger ad agencies have trouble maintaining. R&D Thinktank aims to be a complete advocate: friendly, concerned, forward-thinking.

"This group wanted to do things differently: They are a think tank, coming at the best solutions from all angles, not a traditional studio or ad group," explains Tom Nynas.

A cold, conventional monogram logo or corporate symbol would not be appropriate for this new creative approach. The letters *R&D* also presented their own problems because they could easily be misconstrued to mean "research and development" (they actually stand for Rucker and Deatherage). In the end, the team found the ambiguity a fun double meaning and embraced its possibilities.

Nynas, who at the time of this logo design project was a designer at another studio, considered a number of illustrated solutions that were decidedly unconventional—a light bulb brain, a tank with a thought bubble emerging from its gun, and a light bulb with a fish inside.

"This was a visual client, pretty savvy with respect to what they wanted, so I was able to present a number of unusual ideas," Nynas says.

Interpreting the word *tank* literally seemed to be a promising direction, although the military tank was quickly deemed inappropriate and the fish tank/light bulb felt cliché. So Nynas began thinking about tanks from other angles.

A scuba tank was an intriguing idea. This tank provides life-giving air, and its user is an adventurous explorer. "You need air to survive. An agency survives on ideas. So ideas are an agency's oxygen," Nynas says.

The designer drew an unforgettable and unconventional logo: a scuba diver with a brain as an air tank. The client loved the logo, and the mark soon came to life in other ways. The diver quickly became known as Jacques. Today, R&D has a big fish tank in its office entry. It offers a Jacques Award for employees who embody creative excellence, no matter which discipline they represent within the agency. Account and creative people alike have been recipients of the Jacques Award.

"The logo has really taken on a life of its own that we did not anticipate," says Nynas, who has since been hired by R&D Thinktank as director of design.

A   B   C   D

LOGO SEARCH

Keywords [**Calligraphy**]

Type: ◯ Symbol   ◯ Typographic   ◯ Combo   ⦿ All

 1

 2

 3

 4

 5

Ⓓ = Design Firm   Ⓒ = Client

1C Ⓓ David Kampa Ⓒ Live Oak Brewing Company   1D Ⓓ Brian Collins Design Ⓒ Mimi Dorsey/Fashionrag

2A Ⓓ Novasoul Ⓒ Vaughan   2B Ⓓ Dotzero Design Ⓒ Wrapsody Wraps   2C Ⓓ SKOOTA Ⓒ Harbour Suites   2D Ⓓ Cisneros Design Ⓒ Anasazi Restaurant

3A Ⓓ Novasoul Ⓒ Sandman   3B Ⓓ Sommese Design Ⓒ Sprouts Inc.   3C Ⓓ Novasoul Ⓒ Lavender   3D Ⓓ markatos Ⓒ Disfigure

4A Ⓓ Rotor Design Ⓒ Manitou Free Traders   4B Ⓓ Mattson Creative Ⓒ Taylor Woodrow   4C Ⓓ Weylon Smith Ⓒ Brian and Jannell Barefoot   4D Ⓓ Octavo Designs Ⓒ Sundance Mind & Body Therapy

5A Ⓓ David Kampa Ⓒ Wildcat Records   5B Ⓓ David Kampa Ⓒ Estee Lauder   5C Ⓓ Wray Ward Laseter Ⓒ Seanachai   5D Ⓓ LogoDesignSource.com Ⓒ Fly Label

97

1

firefly

cosmetic café
the spirit of authentic beauty

haute tuna

the
martha's vineyard
african-american
film festival™

2

Sun Tropics®

Jasper's

Fresh™
Get Set for Home Décor

PROVINCIA DE
Buenos Aires

3

ocotillo

Nouveau FiLTH

Schoc
chocolatier

Sukra Yoga

4

Picasso
at the
Lapin Agile

JAZZ

Zoe

5

[Arabic calligraphy logo]

Ⓓ = Design Firm   Ⓒ = Client

1A Ⓓ Felixsockwell.com Ⓒ firefly 1B Ⓓ Insight Design Ⓒ Cosmetic Café 1C Ⓓ judson design associates Ⓒ Haute Tuna 1D Ⓓ adbass:designs LLC Ⓒ cobblestoneentertainment grp.

2A Ⓓ Brandesign Ⓒ Sun Tropics 2B Ⓓ Banowetz + Company, Inc. Ⓒ Kent Rathbun/Jasper's Restaurant 2C Ⓓ Goldforest Ⓒ QEP Co. 2D Ⓓ FutureBrand Ⓒ Buenos Aires Provincial Government

3A Ⓓ Lisa Starace Ⓒ ocotillo 3B Ⓓ Dirty Design Ⓒ Noveau Filth 3C Ⓓ NeoGine Communication Design Ltd Ⓒ Schoc Chocolatier 3D Ⓓ Kendall Ross Ⓒ Sukra Yoga

4A Ⓓ Keyword Design Ⓒ Towle Community Theater 4B Ⓓ FUSZION Collaborative Ⓒ United States Conference of Mayors 4C Ⓓ CONCEPTiCONS Ⓒ Zoe-Miniature Schnauzer 4D Ⓓ Starlight Studio Ⓒ Miranda Movies

5A Ⓓ GSCS Ⓒ UAE royal family 5B Ⓓ Sakkal Design Ⓒ M. Al Meer, Dubai 5C Ⓓ Sakkal Design Ⓒ Hedgebrook Foundation 5D Ⓓ Sakkal Design Ⓒ Tahrir Literary Project

A	B	C	D	

LOGO SEARCH

Keywords `Crests`

Type: ○ Symbol ○ Typographic ○ Combo ● All

1

2

3

4

5

Ⓓ = Design Firm   Ⓒ = Client

1C Ⓓ judson design associates Ⓒ Kountry Bakery   1D Ⓓ sheean design Ⓒ Deutsch/LA Advertising

2A Ⓓ Sayles Graphic Design, Inc. Ⓒ Des Moines Jaycees   2B Ⓓ Parachute Design Ⓒ Lusso Exclusive Residence Collection   2C Ⓓ IMAGEHAUS Ⓒ Ron Beining   2D Ⓓ Colle + McVoy Ⓒ CHS

3A Ⓓ Sockeye Creative Ⓒ adidas   3B Ⓓ Entemotion Design Studio Small Town Treasures   3C Ⓓ Barnstorm Creative Group Inc Ⓒ Mark James Restaurants   3D Ⓓ HMK Archive Ⓒ Mitch Webb & the Swindles

4A Ⓓ Sandstrom Design Ⓒ Full Sail   4B Ⓓ Fauxkoi Ⓒ anodyne bev co.   4C Ⓓ Olson + Company Ⓒ Outdoor Corps   4D Ⓓ R&R Partners Ⓒ Ministry of Productivity

5A Ⓓ Gardner Design Ⓒ Fringe Salon   5B Ⓓ Gardner Design Ⓒ Renewed   5C Ⓓ Gardner Design Ⓒ aspen traders   5D Ⓓ dedstudios Ⓒ ecouture

	A	**B**	**C**	**D**

1

2

3

4

5

Ⓓ = Design Firm   Ⓒ = Client

	A	B	C	D	
1					1
2		PEDDIE SCHOOL			2
3					3
4					4
5					5

	A	B	C	D
1				
2				
3				
4				
5				

Ⓓ = Design Firm   Ⓒ = Client

LOGO SEARCH

Keywords | Sports

Type: ○ Symbol ○ Typographic ○ Combo ● All

	A	B	C	D
1				
2				
3				
4				
5				

D = Design Firm **C** = Client

	A	B	C	D

1

2

3

4

5

Ⓓ = Design Firm   Ⓒ = Client

1A Ⓓ Glitschka Studios Ⓒ Kimberly-Clark Worldwide   1B Ⓓ The Joe Bosack Graphic Design Co. Ⓒ Youngstown Steelhounds   1C Ⓓ Barnstorm Creative Group Inc Ⓒ MayDay Marketing
1D Ⓓ Barnstorm Creative Group Inc Ⓒ Main Events Boxing   2A Ⓓ greteman group Ⓒ pivotal fitness   2B Ⓓ synergy Graphix Ⓒ Spring Brothers   2C Ⓓ o2 ideas Ⓒ Vulcan Run
2D Ⓓ The Clockwork Group Ⓒ North Central Rotary Club/San Antonio   3A Ⓓ Chimera Design Ⓒ Tennis Victoria   3B Ⓓ DDB Dallas Ⓒ Susan G. Komen Breast Cancer Foundation   3C Ⓓ humanot Ⓒ STFC
3D Ⓓ Eyebeam Creative LLC Ⓒ America Scores   4A Ⓓ ComGroup Ⓒ ADT   4B Ⓓ Lars Lawson Ⓒ USA Diving   4C Ⓓ Lars Lawson Ⓒ USA Diving   4D Ⓓ Brainding Ⓒ Western
5A Ⓓ The Joe Bosack Graphic Design co. Ⓒ Unused   5B Ⓓ HMK Archive Ⓒ Randall Mays   5C Ⓓ Ross Hogin Design Ⓒ Cutter & Buck   5D Ⓓ Sayles Graphic Design, Inc. Ⓒ American Athletic Incorporated

Brandia, Lisbon, Portugal

Players in the annual INAS-FID (International Sports Federation for Persons with Intellectual Disability) international football tournament are required to have certain qualifications in addition to superior soccer-playing skills: They must also have doctors' reports attesting to their mental illness or learning disability. Sponsored by two national associations that support those afflicted with mental illness or related disabilities, the tournament is well known in Portugal.

"The Federation is a non-profit whose main purpose is to develop and organize the practice of sports in a competitive environment for Portuguese athletes who bear mental illnesses," explains Miguel Reis, a design director from Brandia, a Lisbon-based design office that was asked to design a logo for the 2003 games.

In 2003, the scope of the games had spread due to testimonials from famous soccer players from around the world. Therefore, the new logo had to express not only the event but its worldwide presence. The notion of different peoples coming together was even more important to note. Not only were people of many nationalities playing together, but so were people of differing disabilities.

"The games have a diversity of cultures, of ways of life and feelings," explains Reis. The designer experimented with silhouettes of people, but this idea was discarded as too open to interpretation. Another idea that was explored was hands in many colors. But this could be interpreted in a patronizing way—that the participants need special help.

"We abandoned that idea because we thought we should emphasize the strongest part of the games, the differences," the designer says.

The solution is a soccer ball that looks as though it could be forming or coming apart. Its many transparent colors play off each other in abstract ways, but the overall shape is still recognizable. The idea is to show dynamism and the many ways a single entity—be it a ball or a person—can be interpreted.

"The concept is that of the importance of each part in the formation of a strong whole. The actual form does not matter; the differences do not matter. The important factor is the clear and transparent way of assuming the differences between each part and its importance in the whole," Reis says.

The logo is powerful and faithful to the concept of the tournament. It is light and transparent in its construction but strong in its final form.

LOGO SEARCH

Keywords **Heads**

Type: ○ Symbol ○ Typographic ○ Combo ● All

1

2

3

4

5

A   B   C   D

	A	B	C	D
1				
2				
3				
4				
5				

Ⓓ = Design Firm Ⓒ = Client

A	B	C	D	
				1
				2
				3
				4
				5

1A ▶ Gardner Design ⒼThe Lone Ranger 1B ▶ concussion, llc Ⓖ buckarooart.com 1C ▶ Jonathan Rice & Company Ⓖ Pharm To Market 1D ▶ Vincent Burkhead Studio Ⓖ the Computer Chef

2A ▶ UlrichPinciotti Design Group Ⓖ Maumee Valley Habitat for Humanity 2B ▶ Glitschka Studios Ⓖ Chaotic Design 2C ▶ KW43 BRANDDESIGN Ⓖ Ritzenhoff AG 2D ▶ Glitschka Studios Ⓖ Studio Presentation

3A ▶ Miaso Design Ⓖ Debutante Riot 3B ▶ Eyebeam Creative LLC Ⓖ Federal Emergency Management Agency 3C ▶ Edward Allen Ⓖ 665 Almost Evil 3D ▶ Edward Allen Ⓖ Words & Music

4A ▶ Edward Allen Ⓖ 665 Almost Evil 4B ▶ CONCEPTiCONS Ⓖ Salvatore 4C ▶ rehab(r) communication graphics Ⓖ rehab(r) communication graphics 4D ▶ TBF Creative Ⓖ Valley Forge

5A ▶ Werner Design Werks Ⓖ media-MINDS, Inc. 5B ▶ UlrichPinciotti Design Group Ⓖ theideakids.com 5C ▶ Doink, Inc. Ⓖ The Modern Stage 5D ▶ The Oesterle Ⓖ The Oesterle

	A	B	C	D
1	 BELLBOY	 Train Your Brain		 CHILDREN'S THEATRE of CHARLOTTE
2	 VINEL FEVER	 Copasetic Custom Clothing Co.	 avantgarb	
3				
4	 Caramelo RESTAURANT	 Virtual Vineyards	 acuity	
5		 ROFILCO	 Confess ? MATIC	

Ⓓ = Design Firm   Ⓒ = Client

1A Ⓓ Bryan Cooper Design Ⓒ Bellboy Records   1B Ⓓ MannPower Design Ⓒ PDI, Inc.   1C Ⓓ Sommese Design Ⓒ Sommese Design   1D Ⓓ Wray Ward Laseter Ⓒ Children's Theatre of Charlotte

2A Ⓓ UNO Ⓒ Vinel Fever   2B Ⓓ Barnstorm Creative Group Inc. Ⓒ Copasetic Clothing Co.   2C Ⓓ Justin Lockwood Design Ⓒ Avant Garb Clothing   2D Ⓓ FUSZION Collaborative Ⓒ Dischord Records

3A Ⓓ Felixsockwell.com Ⓒ AIDS   3B Ⓓ Glitschka Studios Ⓒ Squiggle-Heads   3C Ⓓ Glitschka Studios Ⓒ Squiggle-Heads   3D Ⓓ Glitschka Studios Ⓒ Colored Man Productions

4A Ⓓ Doink, Inc Ⓒ Caramelo Restaurant   4B Ⓓ Gee + Chung Design Ⓒ Virtual Vineyards   4C Ⓓ Werner Design Werks Ⓒ Acuity   4D Ⓓ Glitschka Studios Ⓒ Persona Global

5A Ⓓ Jeff Pollard Design Ⓒ TellThemNow.com   5B Ⓓ Grapefruit Ⓒ Rofilco   5C Ⓓ Werner Design Werks Ⓒ i-Village   5D Ⓓ Turner Duckworth Ⓒ shopping.com

	A	B	C	D	
1					1
2					2
3					3
4					4
5					5

	A	**B**	**C**	**D**
1				
2				
3				
4				
5				

Ⓓ = Design Firm   Ⓒ = Client

Blue Q/Hot & Flashy
Identity and Product Design

Haley Johnson Design, Minneapolis, Minnesota

Haley Johnson Design is a leader in the growing trend of designers working as product creators, not just as product designers. Since the launch of the delectably scented Dirty Girl brand in 1999, the design studio has launched nine successful personal care brands for a single client—Blue Q—the latest of which is Hot & Flashy.

"It was meant to be a menopausal brand," says Haley Johnson, laughing a bit at the notion of creating a design for this niche market. "I was concerned about making this a product line more widely accepted in the gift market. I was uncomfortable focusing totally on menopause, but at the same time I needed to fulfill the desires of the demographic."

Johnson interviewed women in the forty-five- to fifty-five-year-old age group, but it was a twenty-one-year-old niece who really put things into perspective for her. "She told me that sometimes she feels old," the designer recalls. "I realized that no matter the hormone level, every woman needs to be revitalized once in a while. You don't have to be menopausal to need a boost."

For the brand identity, Johnson began by considering what feeling the words *hot* and *flashy* should portray. For the target group,

she decided that letterforms that expressed energy and power would be appropriate. All of Johnson's product designs are highly stylized, usually by time period. For this design, she felt the Art Deco era would be a good match.

"The women of that time appear liberated, sophisticated, and strong in their new-found industrial age. That intrigued me. The richness of the color and design from that period seemed right for the Hot & Flashy demographic, too. It's more mature and opulent, not girly or trendy," she says.

Johnson's typography is an authentic take on the Art Deco period, while its color makes it modern. It and the accompanying graphics are full of contrasts, with plenty of dynamic deco details.

For color, the designer followed the lead of each product. Each item has a unique palette with hot accents and flashy copper metallic foil. For instance, the energy supply kit plays with shades of blue and a spark of yellow. The soap has neutral shades of brown with a hit of lime green.

Overall, the Hot & Flashy identity is cool and confident, just like the women to whom the product is meant to appeal.

A	B	C	D

1

 **LOGO SEARCH**

Keywords **People**

Type: ◯ Symbol ◯ Typographic ◯ Combo ⦿ All

2

  LAS Links

3

4

5

ⓓ = Design Firm   ⓒ = Client

1C ⓓ The Oesterle ⓒ Franzz   1D ⓓ thomas-vasquez.com ⓒ deutsche bank

2A ⓓ Matt Everson Design ⓒ Ogden Plumbing Co.   2B ⓓ Banowetz + Company, Inc. ⓒ Total Mail systems   2C ⓓ Miriello Grafico, Inc. ⓒ CTB/McGraw-Hill   2D ⓓ R&D Thinktank ⓒ AGC

3A ⓓ The Oesterle ⓒ Heidemann   3B ⓓ The Oesterle ⓒ Bodymechanics   3C ⓓ mccoycreative ⓒ Greener Yard Service LLC   3D ⓓ The Oesterle ⓒ Der Ulistrator

4A ⓓ The Oesterle ⓒ Eccomonte   4B ⓓ FUSZION Collaborative ⓒ September Square Communications   4C ⓓ The Oesterle ⓒ Eccomonte   4D ⓓ R&R Partners ⓒ Cowboy Christmas

5A ⓓ Banowetz + Company, Inc. ⓒ Oz Systems   5B ⓓ Element ⓒ Columbus School for Girls   5C ⓓ nicelogo.com ⓒ Sicola martin   5D ⓓ Savage Design Group ⓒ Western Lithograph

	A	**B**	**C**	**D**	
1					1
2					2
3					3
4					4
5					5

Ⓓ = Design Firm   Ⓒ = Client

1A Ⓓ UNO Ⓒ Chivas Regal   1B Ⓓ Hipflix.com Ⓒ Ketone Auto Shop   1C Ⓓ 9MYLES, Inc. Ⓒ RoomKey   1D Ⓓ Sayles Graphic Design, Inc. Ⓒ Duane Tinkey

2A Ⓓ Glitschka Studios Ⓒ ShipITAPO.com   2B Ⓓ Peterson & Company Ⓒ TV Turnoff-Dallas   2C Ⓓ Owen Design Ⓒ UA Local 33   2D Ⓓ Macnab Design Visual Communication Ⓒ Long Now Foundation

3A Ⓓ David Kampa Ⓒ Hungry Eye Studios   3B Ⓓ Gardner Design Ⓒ DanseArte   3C Ⓓ Gardner Design Ⓒ Navential   3D Ⓓ Farah Design, Inc. Ⓒ Vzanz Waxing Center

4A Ⓓ Chimera Design Ⓒ Hydra   4B Ⓓ FUSZION Collaborative Ⓒ Americans for the Arts   4C Ⓓ Mindspace Ⓒ Chrysalis Shelter   4D Ⓓ GSD&M Ⓒ Our Friends Place

5A Ⓓ greteman group Ⓒ pivotal fitness   5B Ⓓ Kevin France Design, Inc. Ⓒ You're Not Alone   5C Ⓓ Ross Hogin Design Ⓒ Live Socket   5D Ⓓ Insight Design Ⓒ My Volunteer Center

	A	B	C	D
1				
2				
3				
4				
5			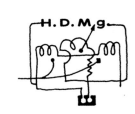	

Ⓓ = Design Firm　Ⓒ = Client

1A Ⓓ greteman group Ⓒ abode　1B Ⓓ Brandia Ⓒ Multicare　1C Ⓓ Strange Ideas Ⓒ coffee icon　1D Ⓓ Catch Design Studio Ⓒ SunSet Bowling

2A Ⓓ greteman group Ⓒ connect west　2B Ⓓ motterdesign Ⓒ Viterma　2C Ⓓ SUMO Ⓒ Science City　2D Ⓓ Landor Associates Ⓒ Lavasa

3A Ⓓ Monster Design Company Ⓒ Now We're Cooking　3B Ⓓ Edward Allen Ⓒ Vespaio Restaurant　3C Ⓓ HMK Archive Ⓒ Igloo Group Austin　3D Ⓓ Stephan and Herr Ⓒ Benny's Bakery

4A Ⓓ Banowetz + Company, Inc. Ⓒ Wall's Catering　4B Ⓓ Designsensory Ⓒ Eddies Pizza　4C Ⓓ Straka Dusan Ⓒ CoFee (Bar/Restaurant)　4D Ⓓ NeoGine Communication Design Ltd Ⓒ Van Dyck Fine Foods

5A Ⓓ Glitschka Studios Ⓒ Kimberly-Clark Worldwide　5B Ⓓ Felixsockwell.com Ⓒ esquire book club　5C Ⓓ Werner Design Werks Ⓒ H.D.M.g.　5D Ⓓ Idle hands Design Ⓒ Drexel

	A	B	C	D
1				
2				
3				
4				
5				

D = Design Firm   **C** = Client

1A D Launchpad Creative C Red Handle Pictures   1B D Paul Black Design C Jensen Magic   1C D 343 Creative C Atlas Welding   1D D Diagram C Strongpage

2A D Formikula C Yakuza Attck Dog-Asian MoviesWebsite   2B D Werner Design Werks C Cameo Beauty Lounge   2C D Launchpad Creative C Isabella   2D D Paul Black Design C Brandye James

3A D Edward Allen C Ranger construction   3B D Edward Allen C Glazing Saddles LTD   3C D Boelts/Stratford Associates C Big Rays Restaurant   3D D Maremar Graphic Design C Bob Leith

4A D Harwood Kirsten Leigh McCoy C Lemnos Dubai   4B D Bryan Cooper Design C WorldCom   4C D Jonathan Rice & Company C Grapevine High School   4D D Formikula C Marc Herold

5A D Vincent Burkhead Studio C Primm & Partners   5B D David Kampa C Pamela Hawthorne   5C D Strange Ideas C stop design theft!   5D D Sabingrafik, Inc. C Settlers Ridge

	A	B	C	D
1				
2				
3				
4				
5				

Ⓓ = Design Firm   Ⓒ = Client

A	B	C	D	
 bARCODE GUYS	 POTHEADS		 JUST CAUZ	1
		 KidsPoint		2
	MILKDRUNK BABY		 seek	3
CONTI GRUP		GLEN BURTNIK'S ROCK ACADEMY	 BandCamp Productions	4
 L E A P	 RON WILLIAMS ORGANIZATION		 HAKS	5

D = Design Firm   **C** = Client

1A **D** joven orozco design **C** Barcode Guys   1B **D** Campbell Fisher Design **C** Pot Heads   1C **D** humanot **C** Unseen Kings   1D **D** Wolken communica **C** Just Cauz

2A **D** DDB Dallas **C** Milton Development Company   2B **D** Communique **C** Foster the Future   2C **D** (twentystar) **C** Colorado Ridge Church   2D **D** zwölf sonnen **C** Peter Kohl

3A **D** Launchpad Creative **C** Daisy Group   3B **D** Monster Design Company **C** Milkdrunk Baby   3C **D** Idle Hands Design **C** Luna Ladder Art for Productions, LLC   3D **D** Glitschka Studios **C** Glitschka Studios

4A **D** Gabi Toth **C** Conti Grup Romania   4B **D** M3 Advertising Design **C** Chris Hammond   4C **D** Studio D **C** Glen Burtnik   4D **D** Who's the Min / Creative Solutions **C** BandCamp Productions

5A **D** Mattson Creative **C** Vital Dynamics   5B **D** i4 Solutions **C** Ron Williams   5C **D** Farm Design **C** Street Jammy Jam Series   5D **D** J6Studios **C** Houston Area Knife Stickers

A	B	C	D

1

2

3

4

5

1

2

3

4

5

ⓓ = Design Firm   ⓒ = Client

1A ⓓ BCM/D ⓒ Scott Mescher   1B ⓓ mixdesign ⓒ T.J. Maloney's   1C ⓓ Dr. Alderete ⓒ Plan 9 store   1D ⓓ CH&LER Design ⓒ By the Cup

2A ⓓ Werner Design Werks ⓒ Cameo Beauty Lounge   2B ⓓ Red Circle ⓒ Stardome Golf Center   2C ⓓ Fresh Oil ⓒ Rhode Runer   2D ⓓ Straka Dusan ⓒ Warner Music/ProSiebenSat.1 Media AG

3A ⓓ www.iseedots.com ⓒ Badhusid   3B ⓓ Werner Design Werks ⓒ TVbyGirls   3C ⓓ R&D Thinktank ⓒ FirstFlight   3D ⓓ Edward Allen ⓒ Upstairs

4A ⓓ Les Kerr Creative ⓒ Visibility, Inc.   4B ⓓ Justin Lockwood Design ⓒ Artattack Theater   4C ⓓ mccoycreative ⓒ Marc Vecco Marine Photography   4D ⓓ Felixsockwell.com ⓒ Coca-Cola

5A ⓓ David Kampa ⓒ Communities in Schools   5B ⓓ Les Kerr Creative ⓒ People Results   5C ⓓ Ammunition ⓒ Weber-Shandwick Worldwide   5D ⓓ 02 ideas ⓒ 94.5

	A	B	C	D
1				
2				
3				
4				
5				

Ⓓ = Design Firm Ⓒ = Client

1A Ⓓ Howerton+White Interactive Ⓒ Maternal Fetal Associates of Kansas 1B Ⓓ Strange Ideas Ⓒ connect mate 1C Ⓓ elf design Ⓒ Weddings 1D Ⓓ Felixsockwell.com Ⓒ AIDS

2A Ⓓ Straka Dusan Ⓒ residential home for the elderly 2B Ⓓ Straka Dusan Ⓒ FirstFootStep 2C Ⓓ BrandSavvy, Inc. Ⓒ Double Angel Foundation 2D Ⓓ FUSZION Collaborative Ⓒ abyan.com

3A Ⓓ Shelley Design + Marketing Ⓒ Parents Anonymous 3B Ⓓ UNO Ⓒ Kimberly Clark 3C Ⓓ traci jones design Ⓒ Hearts for Forgotten Angels 3D Ⓓ Sommese Design Ⓒ Children's Playschool

4A Ⓓ monster design Ⓒ Microsoft Alumni Association 4B Ⓓ Macnab Design Visual Communication Ⓒ Insight Out 4C Ⓓ Kevin France Design, Inc. Ⓒ You're Not Alone 4D Ⓓ o2 ideas Ⓒ Quorum

5A Ⓓ Special Modern Design Ⓒ Flewelling & Moody Architects 5B Ⓓ McAndrew Kaps Ⓒ Associated Pension Service 5C Ⓓ Peterson & Company Ⓒ ERF 5D Ⓓ Lesniewicz Associates Ⓒ Marrow Donor

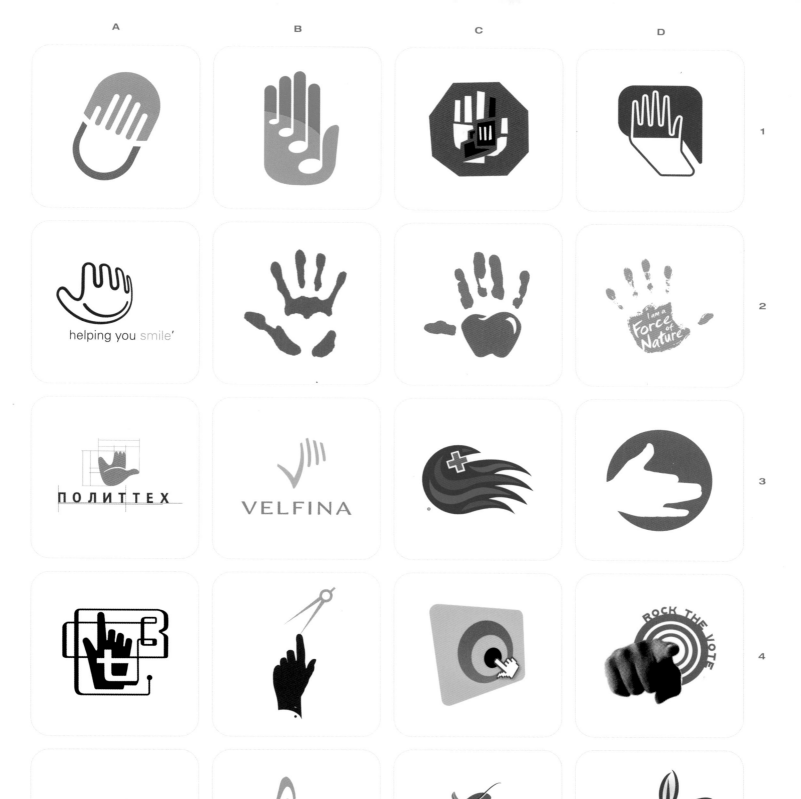

D = Design Firm   **C** = Client

1A **D** Howerton + White Interactive **C** hart   1B **D** Stiles + co **C** Adventure Music/KLIU radio   1C **D** Felixsockwell.com **C** ncayv   1D **D** Gardner Design **C** Russell Public Relations

2A **D** Shift Design **C** BP   2B **D** Oxide Design Co. **C** Nebraska AIDS Project   2C **D** zengigi design **C** Ogilvy PR   2D **D** Edward Allen **C** Force of Nature Organization

3A **D** GRAF d'SIGN creative boutique **C** Polittech   3B **D** Grapefruit **C** Velfina   3C **D** Perfect Circle Media Group **C** Red Cross International   3D **D** o2 ideas **C** Hand in Paw Animal Therapy

4A **D** Werner Design Werks **C** Textbooks.com   4B **D** Polemic Design **C** Expert Construction, LLC   4C **D** Gabriel Kalach * V I S U A L communication **C** Media Targets   4D **D** thomas-vasquez.com **C** Viacom/Rock The Vote

5A **D** Werner Design Werks **C** Media Minds, Inc.   5B **D** nicelogo.com **C** University of Texas   5C **D** Design and Image **C** LifeSpark   5D **D** designlab, inc **C** Spa of Eden

	A	**B**	**C**	**D**
1				
2				
3	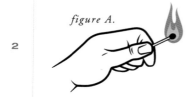			
4				
5				

	A	B	C	D	
1					1
2					2
3					3
4					4
5					5

Ⓓ = Design Firm   Ⓒ = Client

1A Ⓓ Univisual Ⓒ VistaSi 1B Ⓓ Macnab Design Visual Communication Ⓒ Body Wisdom Day Spa 1C Ⓓ mccoycreative Ⓒ HandsOn Salon 1D Ⓓ FigDesign Ⓒ Webb Chiropractic

2A Ⓓ Think Tank Creative Ⓒ Acadiana Open Channel 2B Ⓓ Jenny Kolcun Freelance Designer Ⓒ Ojo Photography 2C Ⓓ Peterson & Company Ⓒ Women's National Book Association 2D Ⓓ Jeff Pollard Design Ⓒ Digitech Solutions

3A Ⓓ Fuego3 Ⓒ Dove Counseling Services 3B Ⓓ Harkey Design Ⓒ Harkey Design 3C Ⓓ FUSZION Collaborative Ⓒ CADCA 3D Ⓓ Glitschka Studios Ⓒ Glitschka Studios

4A Ⓓ Atha Design Ⓒ Oskaloosa Elementary PTO 4B Ⓓ Gabriela Gasparini Design Ⓒ Colby & Partners 4C Ⓓ Glitschka Studios Ⓒ GloveMobile.com 4D Ⓓ Kahn Design Ⓒ Kathy Taylor/Acupuncture & Chinese Herbalist

5A Ⓓ Felixsockwell.com Ⓒ Cigna 5B Ⓓ IMA Design, Corp. Ⓒ Club Portfelio 5C Ⓓ Felixsockwell.com Ⓒ Cigna 5D Ⓓ Idea Girl Design Ⓒ Special Olympics

Operation Seneca
Identity Design

Crescent Lodge, London, United Kingdom

The design team at Crescent Lodge (London) was asked by the Metropolitan Police Service to create a strong yet reassuring identity for Operation Seneca. This strategic initiative is a collaboration of the police and London bus companies that aims to reduce crime levels on the city's public transportation routes.

Information gathered via inward— and outward—facing electronic surveillance equipment on London's buses and police training buses is being used to combat crime and keep the public safe. Named for Lucius Annaeus Seneca, the philosopher and statesman who tried to solve the problems caused by Rome's disaffected youth, the operation, it is hoped, will become associated with public-spirited vigilance.

Designer David Lovelock led the project at Crescent Lodge. "Originally, our idea for the logo was inspired by the welcoming sight of a brightly lit double-decker bus on a dark city night. The shape of the glowing bus windows gives the finished identity its structure. The bus itself remains as unobtrusive as the surveillance undertaken by Operation Seneca."

The logo was given its first airing when the Metropolitan Police Service made a series of presentations to London bus companies

in order to persuade them to become partners in the effort. At this writing, several police training buses bearing Operation Seneca livery are in circulation. Parked at strategic points throughout London, they are helping gather intelligence, facilitate swift responses when crimes are committed, and raise awareness among Londoners of this important initiative.

"The London bus is a familiar, much-loved icon. By turning it into a beacon of light and associating it with a surveillance operation aimed at controlling crime and protecting people, we have created a robust identity that is positive and comforting rather than threatening or oppressive. These days, Londoners are less inclined to object to the growing presence of surveillance cameras anyway, so Operation Seneca and the logo that represents it are very much in tune with the times."

If the success of an initiative like Operation Seneca can be measured by the amount of funding raised to continue its good work, it is worth noting that a state-of-the-art Transport Command Unit is now up and running, thanks to a Transport for London-backed grant of £47 million.

LOGO SEARCH

Keywords **Mythology**

Type: ○ Symbol ○ Typographic ○ Combo ● All

NAUGHTY
&
NICE
COLLECTION

1

INFLUENCE

2

3

4

5

	A	B	C	D
1	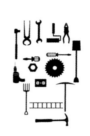			
2				
3				
4				
5				

Ⓓ = Design Firm Ⓒ = Client

1A Ⓓ DDB Ⓒ The Home Depot 1B Ⓓ The Oesterle Ⓒ Spika In Snüzz 1C Ⓓ R&D thinktank Ⓒ Public Executions 1D Ⓓ Rome & Gold Creative Ⓒ Gold Medal Swim Camp

2A Ⓓ Monster Design Company Ⓒ Monster Design Company 2B Ⓓ Ross Hogin Design Ⓒ Storm Hockey Camps 2C Ⓓ Dotzero Design Ⓒ FrightTown 2D Ⓓ FWIS Ⓒ Squarewolf

3A Ⓓ Ammunition Ⓒ Lovechild 3B Ⓓ o2 ideas Ⓒ Vagos Restaurant 3C Ⓓ markatos Ⓒ Disfigure 3D Ⓓ Special Modern Design Ⓒ Jennifer Diamond Foundation

4A Ⓓ Olson + Company Ⓒ The Basilica of St. Mary 4B Ⓓ concussion, llc Ⓒ Recommended Foods, Inc. 4C Ⓓ Lisa Starace Ⓒ all my sons 4D Ⓓ The Meyocks Group Ⓒ Two Saints

5A Ⓓ Pixel Basement Ⓒ Tav Shande 5B Ⓓ R&D Thinktank Ⓒ Delta Medics 5C Ⓓ Gardner Design Ⓒ ESSFA 5D Ⓓ Macnab Design Visual Communication Ⓒ Angela Buono

	A	B	C	D	

1

2

3

4

5

Ⓓ = Design Firm   Ⓒ = Client

1A Ⓓ CAPSULE Ⓒ Myth Nightclub   1B Ⓓ McAndrew Kaps Ⓒ Wavecode   1C Ⓓ Gardner Design Ⓒ Spirit Aerosystems   1D Ⓓ Tactical Magic Ⓒ Fulmer Helmets

2A Ⓓ Hinge Ⓒ Internet2   2B Ⓓ ivan2design Ⓒ Kharakat   2C Ⓓ Harkey Design Ⓒ Griffin Company   2D Ⓓ David Kampa Ⓒ Horsefeathers Trading Company

3A Ⓓ Quest Fore Ⓒ GlaxoSmithKline   3B Ⓓ Element Ⓒ Columbus School for Girls   3C Ⓓ Diagram Ⓒ ING Real Estate Development   3D Ⓓ Sergio Bianco Ⓒ Incisori Fiorentini

4A Ⓓ Idle Hands Design Ⓒ Ouroboros Ink   4B Ⓓ Turner Duckworth Ⓒ S.A. Brain & Co. Ltd   4C Ⓓ Glitschka Studios Ⓒ Body Glove-Asia   4D Ⓓ Studio Simon Ⓒ Golden Baseball League

5A Ⓓ the atmosfear Ⓒ MGM MIRAGE   5B Ⓓ www.iseedots.com Ⓒ NovaStor   5C Ⓓ sheean design Ⓒ Maddocks & Co.   5D Ⓓ Sommese Design Ⓒ Penn State Jazz Club

129

A	B	C	D

1

2

3

4

5

Bravo Network
Identity Redesign

Open, New York, New York

Bravo is the only television network whose name makes a statement. It's something one might actually say out loud, particularly in response to the arts programming it carried at its inception some twenty years ago.

Its logo was a straightforward affair until recently, when Open (New York City) redesigned it as part of an overall redesign of the network. Since NBC bought Bravo in 2003, the network has gone through a series of changes.

Bravo used to be a general arts channel, with movies, interviews with authors, concerts—a PBS that wasn't PBS, explains Scott Stowell, the proprietor of Open. "Since NBC took over, they've run shows like *Queer Eye for the Straight Guy, Celebrity Poker Showdown,* and reruns of *West Wing.* It's a real hodgepodge," he says.

More recently, Bravo has added original shows like the popular *Project Runway*, and a tagline, "Watch what happens," that celebrates the variety of programming on the network. So the Bravo logo had to make a statement, too, expressing the reaction to seeing something surprising and great.

The Canadian version of Bravo has an exclamation point at the end of its wordmark. It was a small jump for the designers to add a word bubble to the U.S. version. "It was an obvious idea," Stowell says, "but the response from the client was positive."

But getting to the final logo took a lot more fine-tuning. Color and type studies were conducted for weeks and weeks. The new logo had to look fresh but be similar enough to the original mark that loyal viewers would feel comfortable with it. Tobias Frere-Jones of Hoefler & Frere-Jones Typography drew the type for the final logo.

The shape of the word bubble required its own set of extensive studies. "Our favorite version was a rectangle. One of the client's mandates was to attract more male viewers—hence, the hard, angled shape. But Bravo felt that might be too generic, and they asked that we make a shape that could be more specific," Stowell says.

After many experiments with shapes, corners, line weight, and so on, Bravo president Lauren Zalaznick asked that the designers try placing two rounded corners on one end and two right angles on the other. It worked, both as an effective word bubble shape and as a strong identifier. The final design is definitely specific to Bravo.

Stowell feels the logo succeeds because it is so simple. It's what it is supposed to be. "It fulfills the requirements of a classic logo. It's not 3-D or made of metal or translucent. It can be run in a flat color or stitched onto a baseball hat or silkscreened onto a shirt. Many logos today are more like illustrations because they're so complicated," he adds. "This one works really well inside the busy environment of TV."

(Top) New design
(Bottom) Old design

A | B | C | D

Row 1

LOGO SEARCH

Keywords: Birds

Type: ○ Symbol ○ Typographic ○ Combo ● All

Row 2

Row 3

Row 4

Row 5

Ⓓ = Design Firm   Ⓒ = Client

1C Ⓓ Peters Design Ⓒ Messier-Bugatti-Tracer 1D Ⓓ Moonsire Ⓒ Contract Associates

2A Ⓓ The Joe Bosack Graphic Design Co. Ⓒ ECHL 2B Ⓓ Jeff Pollard Design Ⓒ Nike 2C Ⓓ Ross Hogin Design Ⓒ Seattle Thunderbirds 2D Ⓓ Barnstorm Creative Group Inc. Ⓒ Carson Air Flight Centres

3A Ⓓ Peterson & Company Ⓒ Eagle Materials Inc. 3B Ⓓ Walsh Associates Ⓒ Seahawk Rubber Ring Manufacturing 3C Ⓓ AKOFA Creative Ⓒ Self Promotional 3D Ⓓ Scott Oeschger Design Ⓒ Saint Joseph's Preparatory School

4A Ⓓ greteman group Ⓒ Raven Café 4B Ⓓ Sommese Design Ⓒ State College Park Preservation 4C Ⓓ Typonic Ⓒ Spielerabe 4D Ⓓ Werner Design Werks Ⓒ Grand Connect

5A Ⓓ sarah watson design Ⓒ Darby James 5B Ⓓ Mohouse Design Co. Ⓒ Bright 5 Productions, LLC. 5C Ⓓ Studio Stubborn Sideburn Ⓒ Saiwai Law Firm 5D Ⓓ Cato Purnell Partners Ⓒ Hiranandani Group

	A	B	C	D	

A	B	C	D

JARDINI (C1)

1

 **MINE™**

2

3

4

5

⏺ = Design Firm ⏷ = Client

	A	B	C	D
1				
2				
3				
4				
5				

D = Design Firm **C** = Client

1A **D** R&D thinktank **C** AwakeTel 1B **D** Steven O'Connor **C** chicken 1C **D** Gardner Design **C** Backroads Traveler 1D **D** Colle + McVoy **C** Ciatti's Chianti Grill

2A **D** ivan2design **C** El Pollo Loco 2B **D** Morse and Company Advertising Communications **C** Cyrano's Restaurant 2C **D** Element **C** Howe Family Reunion 2005 2D **D** Whence: the studio **C** The Krewe of Wild Turkeys

3A **D** KONG Design Group **C** Listen Skateboards 3B **D** Rick Johnson & Company **C** Quail Ranch 3C **D** Dashwood Design Ltd **C** Farrow Jamieson 3D **D** Sandstrom Design **C** White Owl

4A **D** Bright Strategic Design **C** Paradise on a Hanger 4B **D** Gardner Design **C** Bradley Paper 4C **D** Gardner Design **C** Bradley Paper 4D **D** Fernandez Design **C** Kiwi

5A **D** McGuire Design **C** Denise Swanson 5B **D** Gardner Design **C** City of Newton, KS 5C **D** Michael Courtney Design, Inc. **C** Maggie Martin, Midwife 5D **D** Mires **C** Pelican Video Games

LOGO SEARCH

Keywords: **Fish/Bugs/Reptiles**

Type: ◯ Symbol   ◯ Typographic   ◯ Combo   ⦿ All

1

2

3

4

5

A	**B**	**C**	**D**

1

2

3

4

5

Ⓓ = Design Firm Ⓒ = Client

	A	B	C	D	
1			 beyond blue	 COUNTINGCROWS	
2		 THE ART STATION Growth & Healing Through the Creative Arts	 BETTER ATM	
3		STINGERS	QUEEN BEE TAKING THE STING OUT OF WAXING waxing	 Have Wax, Will Travel
4	 BUSY BEE TAILORING		 buzzsaw.com	
5		 Dragonfly		 GOODNIGHT EXTERMINATORS

Skywest
Identity Design

Cato Purnell, Sydney and Melbourne, Australia

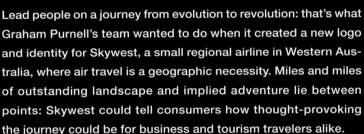

Lead people on a journey from evolution to revolution: that's what Graham Purnell's team wanted to do when it created a new logo and identity for Skywest, a small regional airline in Western Australia, where air travel is a geographic necessity. Miles and miles of outstanding landscape and implied adventure lie between points: Skywest could tell consumers how thought-provoking the journey could be for business and tourism travelers alike.

"We wanted to push the boundaries for the client and for the traveler," says Purnell, creative director of Cato Purnell Partners, Sydney and Melbourne.

Skywest had to deal with stiff competition from better-known airlines such as Virgin Blue. But it also had the opportunity to move into dead center and deliver a more emotional message, one that was unique to the feeling of being in Australia.

Purnell's team started with givens: the client's name and choice of color, which really had to be a sky blue.

"Skywest is a great name. We wanted the new identity to open up the concept of *sky.* In Western Australia, there is this broad expanse of sky," Purnell says. He and his designers developed a frame element roughly 3.5 times wider than it is tall that is a crucial part of the new identity. In it, the blue sky can appear, or panoramic shots from any Skywest destination can be dropped in. "The box is iconic and strong on its own. It is a revolutionary concept of panorama."

Another important part of the new identity is a sunburst. "When you look out the plane window, you often see this sunflower light on the glass. The sunburst element is distinctive and new in the industry. Now, they can take a panoramic shot of a tourist destination, put it in the frame, then stamp it with the sunburst in order to take ownership, so to speak, of the destination," Purnell explains.

LOGO SEARCH

Keywords | **Animals**

Type: ○ Symbol ○ Typographic ○ Combo ◉ All

1

UNDERDOG
ANIMATION

bowhouse

BraggingRightsonline
"It Pays To Be The Top Dog"

2

doglogic
AGILITY TRAINING

3

THE PALMS
PET RESORT & SPA

★ BROADBAND
bingo

jackpoint
pontos surpresa para o seu cartão fast

4

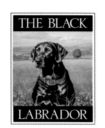
the bone
BISTRO

THE BLACK
LABRADOR

STUMPTOWN
PORTER

5

	A	B	C	D
1				
2				
3				
4				
5				

A | B | C | D

 FOX FIELD COMMUNITY

 FOX CHASE HOMEOWNERS · ASSOCIATION *Philadelphia*

 LONE WOLF ENERGY

 MTILDA

1

 Phoenix ZOO

2

 WILD GAME

3

 mini doe

 CORNERSTONE

 Rocky Mountain Elk Foundation

4

 Erie Bleu Alpaca Farm

 HORSEPOWER

 RED FENCE Farm

 WILDWOOD HILLS RANCH

5

	A	B	C	D
1				
2				
3				
4				
5				

Ⓓ = Design Firm   Ⓒ = Client

1A Ⓓ Campbell Fisher Design Ⓒ Wildfire Golf   1B Ⓓ Fresh Oil Ⓒ Chester's Chophouse & Wine Bar   1C Ⓓ The Joe Bosack Graphic Design Co. Boise State   1D Ⓓ GSCS Ⓒ Madinat Jumeirah

2A Ⓓ Hubbell Design Works Ⓒ Surf & Spa Stables   2B Ⓓ Macnab Design Visual Communication Ⓒ Maddoux-Wey Arabians   2C Ⓓ Edward Allen Ⓒ Half Moon Farm   2D Ⓓ Kendall Creative Shop, Inc. Ⓒ Bank of America

3A Ⓓ S Design, Inc. Ⓒ The Coach House   3B Ⓓ Whitney Edwards LLC Ⓒ Biga Fund   3C Ⓓ Brandia Ⓒ CTT Correios   3D Ⓓ UNO Ⓒ Circo America

4A Ⓓ Jeff Pollard Design Ⓒ Hay Processing Unlimited   4B Ⓓ sarah watson design Ⓒ Laughing Horse Theatre   4C Ⓓ R&D Thinktank Ⓒ Nynas Strategic Design   4D Ⓓ Steven O'Connor Ⓒ Democratic Party

5A Ⓓ Howerton+White Interactive Ⓒ Buffalo Saints   5B Ⓓ Studio Simon Ⓒ Harpeth Indians   5C Ⓓ Brainding Ⓒ Bife   5D Ⓓ Fresh Oil Ⓒ Blackstone Studios

A	B	C	D	
				1
				2
				3
				4
				5

	A	**B**	**C**	**D**
1				
2				
3				
4				
5				

Domaine Restaurants Ltd.
Identity Design

Ramp Creative, Los Angeles, California

The logo and identity system for Domaine Restaurants Ltd., a holding company in Orange County, California, that owns and creates progressive and highly regarded restaurants, is an excellent example of a successful compromise.

Ramp Creative, Los Angeles, was the design firm that achieved the bargain. Principals Michael Stinson and Rachel Elnar met with Domaine owners Tim and Liza Goodell, who together have founded nationally recognized restaurants such as Meson G, Troquet, and Aubergine. Right away, the designers saw that the partners could easily head in different directions in their new identity. Tim, a talented French chef, loved traditional concepts. Liza, on the other hand, wanted a modern design, full of color and personality.

Stinson and Elnar did design experiments that ranged from pole to pole—traditional to modern—but they soon discovered that the two could be blended, much to the pleasure of the clients. The logo solution was a traditional, illuminated letterform, a combination of a D and an R intertwined with vines and ivy.

"The mark is ornate, like ivy climbing over a passageway opening in France, leading to a tunnel that goes into a vineyard," says Stinson.

But the way the logo was implemented in the identity was very modern. On one side of Domaine's calling card-sized business cards (2 ½" x 3 ½" [6.35 x 8.89 cm]) is the engraved logo on a chocolate-brown field. But on the other side is a bright mint-green field with the card carrier's contact information. Other pieces in the system carried other bright colors.

"We did a whole palette for them. The rest of the stationery utilized a salmon color for the envelopes and a lime green for the letterheads. The company folders' neutral palette accommodated the bright colors used inside as well as on the website. The brown color ties everything together; it allows all the colors in the system to be joined by this neutral color," explains Stinson. This flexibility is important because Domaine operates many styles of restaurant, traditional and contemporary. The identity must serve as an accommodating umbrella for all of them.

The ivy element in the logo turned out to be another contemporary element on Domaine's website (www.domainerestaurants.com). Ramp Creative animated the tendrils so they wind and twine on different pages. But rather than displayed in black or a solid color, they are transparent, allowing new images to show through from behind. The effect obscures and reveals at the same time. Ramp even shot all the imagery that appears on the website to ensure the visuals coordinated with the modern feel of the site.

"When we first met with Tim and Liza, they argued like two chefs. They definitely had two different styles, but this blend works for them both," Stinson says.

LOGO SEARCH

Keywords **Nature**

Type: ○ Symbol ○ Typographic ○ Combo ● All

Tsb
Trusted Sugar Brands

MINT
get fresh with your career

A	B	C	D	
	 essentials MIND BODY & SOUL		 TODD A. FRANKLIN, D.D.S.	1
 VRAITERRE	 OLD TOWN TEA CO.	 LEIGH HOWELL LOVE LANDSCAPE DESIGN INC.	THE ENRICHMENT PROJECT creating growth and opportunity	2
 SAGE THEATRE GROUP	 PrairieStone pharmacy	FALL STYLE SHOWCASE		3
 idp	 Changing Colors Fall Festivals of Central New York	 TOBACCO CAFE•COM	 agave™	4
	 macore	 svärmisk	 TWIN OAKS MARINE & SPORT	5

Ⓓ = Design Firm   Ⓒ = Client

1A Ⓓ UlrichPinciotti Design Group Ⓒ Otsego Schools   1B Ⓓ Polkadot Ⓒ Advanced Clinical Systems   1C Ⓓ octane inc. Ⓒ Renewable Energy Resources   1D Ⓓ Monster Design Company Ⓒ Todd A. Franklin, DDS
2A Ⓓ Design One Ⓒ Vraiterre   2B Ⓓ Octavo Designs Ⓒ Old Town Tea Co.   2C Ⓓ Visual Inventor Ltd. Co. Ⓒ Leigh Howell Love   2D Ⓓ ginger griffin marketing and design Ⓒ The Enrichment Project
3A Ⓓ Peterson & Company Ⓒ sage theatre group   3B Ⓓ CAPSULE Ⓒ Prairie Stone Pharmacy   3C Ⓓ Freshwater Design Ⓒ North Hills   3D Ⓓ Glitschka Studios Ⓒ Cardwell Creative
4A Ⓓ Cato Purnell Partners Ⓒ IDP   4B Ⓓ GrafiQa Graphic Design Ⓒ NYSHA   4C Ⓓ KOESTER design Ⓒ TobaccoCafe.com   4D Ⓓ INNFUSION Studios Ⓒ Agave Films
5A Ⓓ Modern Dog Design Co. Ⓒ Newport Corporate   5B Ⓓ Glitschka Studios Ⓒ Macore Company   5C Ⓓ Chimera Design Ⓒ Svarmisk   5D Ⓓ IMAGEHAUS Ⓒ Twin Oaks Marine

	A	B	C	D

A   **B**   **C**   **D**

1

Kansas Stars

ZŁOTE TARASY

Bubel Aiken
foundation

2

agave

love.com

3

SUNJOI

NUANSA ASRI CIPADU

4

DAILYcolors™

BOTANIA

North American Biomass Corporation

5

INN AT BEVERLY HILLS

CORHAM

PROSPECT
PLACE
apartments

PICO
MACCARIO

A **B**   **C** **D**

POPPYSEED CAKE
INVITATIONS · CARDS

FRANCE JACMAIN
STYLIST

jardín

1

idlewild
jewelry design

CASTLEWOOD
at BIG SKY

Каракулино
Молоко ®

2

seed™

Europharm

EUROCATALYST
EVERYBODY WINS

3

RIGHTEOUS BEAN
A GREAT COFFEE, A GREAT CAUSE

GOURMONDO
the art of food

CONIFER
PURVEYORS of SPECIALTY FOODS

4

THE LONE RANGER COLLECTION

Asah Terra

5

Ⓓ = Design Firm   Ⓒ = Client

1A Ⓓ elf design Ⓒ Poppyseed Cake   1B Ⓓ Ardoise Design Ⓒ Immotik inc.   1C Ⓓ GetElevatedDesign.com Ⓒ Green Lotus Grounds   1D Ⓓ Lisa Starace Ⓒ jardín
2A Ⓓ baba designs Ⓒ Enchanted Minstrel Music   2B Ⓓ The Pink Pear Design Company Ⓒ Idlewild Jewelry Design   2C Ⓓ Mattson Creative Ⓒ Shea Homes   2D Ⓓ design-studio Muhina Ⓒ Karakulino Milk
3A Ⓓ seed Ⓒ seed   3B Ⓓ Brandient Ⓒ GlaxoSmithKline   3C Ⓓ Imaginaria Ⓒ Azteca Milling   3D Ⓓ HMK Archive Ⓒ euroCatalyst
4A Ⓓ Rickabaugh Graphics Ⓒ Mountain View Coffee Roasters   4B Ⓓ Methodologie Ⓒ Gourmondo Catering   4C Ⓓ zwölf sonnen Ⓒ Förderverein Fachhochschule Wiesbaden   4D Ⓓ Brand Navigation Ⓒ Conifer Specialties
5A Ⓓ Gardner Design Ⓒ The Lone Ranger   5B Ⓓ The Flores Shop Ⓒ The Cedarhouse School   5C Ⓓ Richards Brock Miller Mitchell & Associates Ⓒ The Home Depot   5D Ⓓ Curtis Sharp Design Ⓒ Asah Terra

A	B	C	D

1

2

3

4

5

ⓓ = Design Firm ⓒ = Client

1A ⓓ OmniStudio Inc ⓒ Modern Africa 1B ⓓ Ramp ⓒ compLife 1C ⓓ Hinge ⓒ Bonsai Labs 1D ⓓ Miriello Grafico, Inc. ⓒ Barratt American

2A ⓓ Mohouse Design Co. ⓒ Lakewood Service League 2B ⓓ Actual Size Creative ⓒ Shady Grove 2C ⓓ Napoleon design ⓒ APAE-Associação de Pais e Amigos dos Excepcionais-Bauru 2D ⓓ Sibley Peteet ⓒ Sanders\Wingo

3A ⓓ www.iseedots.com ⓒ Orchard Group, Inc. 3B ⓓ The Collaboration ⓒ City of Glendale 3C ⓓ The Robin Shepherd Group ⓒ Earth Day 3D ⓓ Diagram ⓒ Plantec

4A ⓓ Felixsockwell.com ⓒ Cigna 4B ⓓ Simon & Goetz Design ⓒ Elenxis 4C ⓓ Brandia ⓒ BancoBIC 4D ⓓ christiansen : creative ⓒ liveliberal.org

5A ⓓ joe miller's company ⓒ Shade 5B ⓓ the zen kitchen ⓒ Branches Fine Gifts 5C ⓓ concussion, llc ⓒ Treehouse Foods, Inc. 5D ⓓ judson design associates ⓒ Chinquapin School

	A	B	C	D
1				

	A	B	C	D
1				
2				
3				
4				
5			—	—

Froggy
Identity Redesign

Zebra Design Branding, Togliatti, Russia

Froggy is a Russian computer product that allows customers to order new computers à la carte—that is, users tell a Froggy specialist what they want to do with the computer, and the specialist pulls together the most appropriate configuration using parts from leading component manufacturers, including Intel and Samsung. Users can also decide how much power their computer needs, selecting from one of five comprehensive RAM levels.

Froggy, a division of IVS Group in Perm, is known as a friendly brand, ideal for the person who wants to use a computer for games, the Internet, and word processing but who knows little about electronics. The company's old logo had a friendly enough look: a smiling, T-shirt-wearing cartoon frog that sat still for print applications and was animated for electronic media. Once only a home computer brand, Froggy moved into the business market as well, and the old logo was no longer appropriate.

The client even wondered if the company name should be changed. But Andrey Mitin, art director of Zebra Brand Marketing (Togliatti, Russia) didn't think so. "In our opinion, the name Froggy is the most accurate way to show the character of this brand, its essence. A froggy is a kind and positive character. It is never mischievous or troublesome, nor are Froggy computers," he says.

Still, Mitin and his designers wanted to address the client's concerns about whether or not a frog was too whimsical for its expanding business. So they dissected the frog, so to speak, and considered elements of the creature that would reflect the company's friendly nature yet be decidedly more corporate.

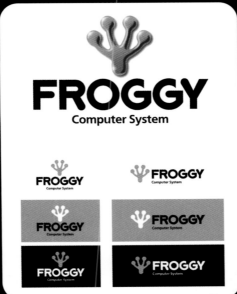

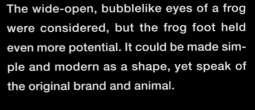

The wide-open, bubblelike eyes of a frog were considered, but the frog foot held even more potential. It could be made simple and modern as a shape, yet speak of the original brand and animal.

"The basic meaning of the new logo is as a helping hand the froggy stretches out to everyone in a complicated computer world," explains Mitin. "Alongside the primary meaning, this logo can also be looked at as a tree—a principle of computer systemizing—or microcircuit contacts. Some people even see the famous USB symbol in it."

Using the color orange made the frog foot even more distinctive, as frogs this color are exotic and rare. The orange is unexpected and memorable. The bright, positive color is also a strong differentiating factor that distinguishes Froggy from duller, more corporate rivals.

The new brand positioning statement—"Play. Learn. Think. Work. Win!"—was released at the same time as the logo (in fact, it can sit right inside the new logo), and both have been a hit, and not just with customers. In February 2005, the Froggy brand earned the right to carry Microsoft's "Designed for Windows" statement on its products and packaging. The new identity was also ranked in the top ten of the best-rated corporate identities in Russia for 2005.

The new logo and identity immediately received positive public reaction. Contact with the brand is much more pleasant, for customers and staff. Since the new launch, Froggy has attracted more corporate customers and has extended its segment of home users. Rebranding helped the company become a leader in the personal computer market in Perm, says Mitin.

LOGO SEARCH

Keywords | **Shapes**

Type: ○ Symbol   ○ Typographic   ○ Combo   ◉ All

ASSURANT

BankDirect

WORLDWIDE OPERATIONS

grupo H

x·cursion

AIRWAVE

MUNDO SPORTING
VIAGEM AO UNIVERSO LEONINO

PURL.

Centigon

TerryWhite chemists

OCEANIA

4° INAS-FID
Campeonato de Futebol
EURO'03

Davidson Oil

Ⓓ = Design Firm   Ⓒ = Client

1C Ⓓ Carbone Smolan Agency Ⓒ Assurant 1D Ⓓ Cato Purnell Partners Ⓒ Bank Direct

2A Ⓓ David Kampa Ⓒ David Carter Design 2B Ⓓ Gee + Chung Design Ⓒ Sun Microsystems 2C Ⓓ Brainding Ⓒ grupo H 2D Ⓓ Gardner Design Ⓒ X-Cursion

3A Ⓓ Strategy Studio Ⓒ International Resource Center 3B Ⓓ R&R Partners Ⓒ Airwave 3C Ⓓ Fernandez Design Ⓒ Citrix 3D Ⓓ Brandia Ⓒ Sporting Clube de Portugal

4A Ⓓ switchfoot creative Ⓒ Conquest Trading Co. 4B Ⓓ Landor Associates Ⓒ Centigon 4C Ⓓ Cato Purnell Partners Ⓒ Terry White Chemists 4D Ⓓ Strange Ideas Ⓒ Oceania

5A Ⓓ Brandia Ⓒ INAS FID 5B Ⓓ Thomas Manss & Company Ⓒ VCC Perfect Pictures 5C Ⓓ Shift design Ⓒ SDNM 5D Ⓓ tanagram partners Ⓒ Davidson Oil

	A	B	C	D	

Optimum online

1

Simple
Software Training

tapspace creativity in percussion

REYES MARKETING

EQUITYMOMENTUM

2

Hydro Power

mood boost

Gforce

3

unison

4

MUSE 2005
Metropolitan University Scholar's Experience

ideal
exposure

5

D = Design Firm   C = Client

1A D Sterling Brands C Cablevision 1B D Gee Creative C Turnkey Technology Solutions 1C D Mindspace C Omnilink Systems 1D D www.iseedots.com C Snackmoney Records

2A D Joi Design C Simple Software Training 2B D Dialekt Design C Tapspace Publications 2C D Fox Parlor C Lita Reyes 2D D Barnstorm Creative C Equity Momentum

3A D Land Design C Pulte Homes, Inc. 3B D Paragon Design International C Chicago Harbors 3C D Brandia C Ola 3D D Brandia C Galp Energia

4A D Dashwood Design Ltd C Unison 4B D Ross Hogin Design C Paragon Media 4C D Ikola designs... C Sunstar Foods 4D D BLOOM LLC C BLOOM

5A D Gardner Design C New Horizon 5B D Living Creative Design C San José State University 5C D Brainding C Ideal Exposure 5D D mattisimo C coastal surfwear

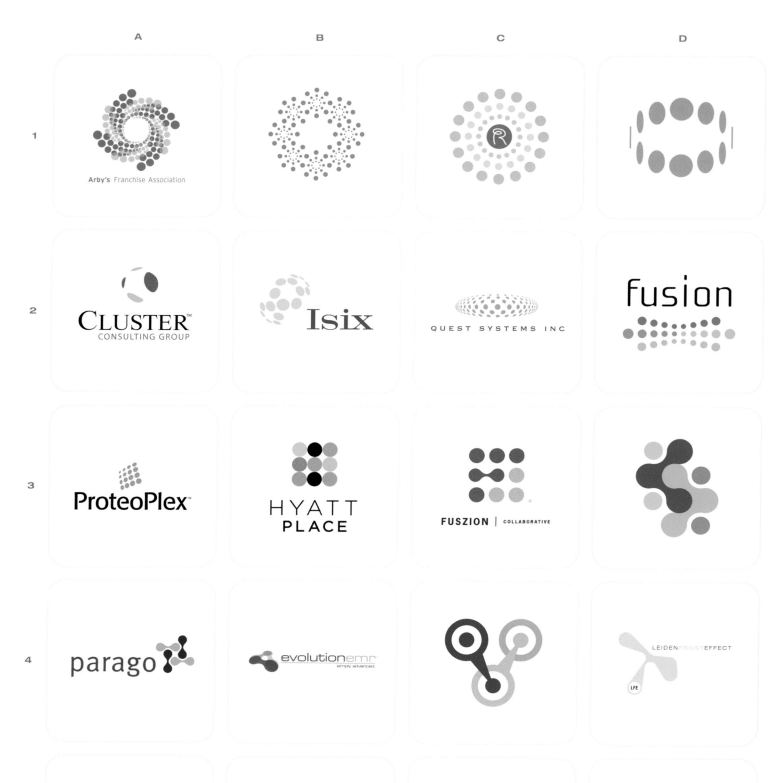

Arby's Franchise Association

CLUSTER™
CONSULTING GROUP

Isix

QUEST SYSTEMS INC

fusion

ProteoPlex™

HYATT
PLACE

FUSZION | COLLABORATIVE

parago

evolutionemr
simply advanced.

LEIDENFROSTEFFECT

LFE

bump
networks

plusinfinite

mediaengine

InternalMonologue

A	B	C	D	
 POLYSHELL	  Listen In	 goosebumps	 Valence Health	1
	 Netigy™		 cognistar	2
	 Cálidda GAS NATURAL DEL PERÚ		 Nowiejski 401(k) Associates, LP	3
			 star peer tutoring programme	4
	 pfi. Pink Films International			5

Ⓓ = Design Firm Ⓒ = Client

1A Ⓓ elaine park Ⓒ Akina Inc. 1B Ⓓ bunch Ⓒ Listen In–Portugal 1C Ⓓ Kaimere Ⓒ Goosebumps Records 1D Ⓓ tanagram partners Ⓒ Valence Health

2A Ⓓ Kym Abrams Design Ⓒ Montgomery Ward /Mobil 2B Ⓓ Gee + Chung Design Ⓒ Netigy Corporation 2C Ⓓ A3 Design Ⓒ New Jack Soul 2D Ⓓ Lippincott Mercer Ⓒ Cognistar

3A Ⓓ FutureBrand Ⓒ Buenos Aires Province Government 3B Ⓓ FutureBrand Ⓒ Tractebel Peru 3C Ⓓ Brian Blankenship Ⓒ Jetta 3D Ⓓ Steven O'Connor Ⓒ Nowiejski 401(k) Associates, LP

4A Ⓓ Braue; Branding & Corporate Design Ⓒ Concore 4B Ⓓ Maremar Graphic Design Ⓒ Abbott Laboratories 4C Ⓓ Letter 7 Ⓒ SixPointStudios 4D Ⓓ Axiom Design Partners Ⓒ STAR Peer Tutoring Programme

5A Ⓓ Landor Associates Ⓒ FedEx Kinko's 5B Ⓓ Unibrand Belgrade Ⓒ pink film Ⓓ Steven O'Connor Ⓒ EZLN 5D Ⓓ S Design, Inc. Ⓒ Thinking Cap/Oklahoma Partnership for School Readiness

	A	**B**	**C**	**D**

1

2

3

4

5

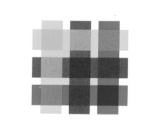   

Ⓓ = Design Firm   Ⓒ = Client

1A Ⓓ Gabriela Gasparini Design Ⓒ Miracle Mind 1B Ⓓ thomas-vasquez.com Ⓒ Book Forum-Frankfurt, Germany 1C Ⓓ Brand Navigation Ⓒ City Bible Church 1D Ⓓ Eisenberg and Associates Ⓒ Systemware

2A Ⓓ Unibrand Belgrade Ⓒ Naftagas 2B Ⓓ Brandia Ⓒ Câmara Municipal de Oeiras 2C Ⓓ Dirty Design Ⓒ Optimum Mastering 2D Ⓓ Eisenberg and Associates Ⓒ Systemware 3A Ⓓ Diagram Ⓒ ING Real Estate Development

3B Ⓓ Mindspace Ⓒ Destinator Technologies 3C Ⓓ Dan Rood Design Ⓒ China Pathway Logistics 3D Ⓓ Cato Purnell Partners Ⓒ Guangzhou Baiyun International Airport 4A Ⓓ Carbone Smolan Agency Ⓒ Brooklyn Botanic Garden

4B Ⓓ Lippincott Mercer Ⓒ First Citizens Bank 4C Ⓓ Brandient Ⓒ Romanian National Radio Communications Society SA 4D Ⓓ Onoma, LLC Ⓒ Diversity Initiative Group for LeBoeuf, Lam, Green & MacRae LLP

5A Ⓓ Cato Purnell Partners Ⓒ Infratil 5B Ⓓ Polemic Design Ⓒ Sophistication by Roseanne Bianchetta 5C Ⓓ MANMADE Ⓒ Family Geometries 5D Ⓓ Thomas Manss & Company Ⓒ Oberhavel Holding

158

	A	B	C	D
1				
2				
3				
4				
5				

D = Design Firm **C** = Client

1A **D** Sandstrom Design **C** Surround Architects   1B **D** Kendall Ross **C** Precept Brands   1C **D** NeoGine Communication Design Ltd **C** Paragee   1D **D** Cheri Gearhart, graphic design **C** Sarah's Inn

2A **D** Polemic Design **C** Proposal   2B **D** Jeff Pollard Design **C** Cornish College of the Arts   2C **D** Lippincott Mercer **C** The Bank of New York   2D **D** Cato Purnell Partners **C** Clearview

3A **D** Kineto **C** PT Karya Deka Pancamurni   3B **D** Gardner Design **C** The Chapel   3C **D** Brandia **C** RadioTelevisão Portuguesa   3D **D** 28 LIMITED BRAND **C** Schleupen AG

4A **D** Gardner Design **C** Spirit Aerosystems   4B **D** Visual Coolness **C** Experience Analysts International   4C **D** Gardner Design **C** Spirit Aerosystems   4D **D** Dashwood Design Ltd **C** The EDGE

5A **D** Mirko Ilic Corp **C** Broadmoor Engineering   5B **D** Barnstorm Creative **C** Camelot Consulting   5C **D** FutureBrand **C** InBest Forex   5D **D** Grapefruit **C** UCS Romania

	A	B	C	D
1				
2				
3				
4				
5				

A B C D

LOGO SEARCH

Keywords: **Symbols**

Type: ⊙ Symbol   ⊙ Typographic   ⊙ Combo   ⦿ All

crave
CHOCOLATIER

Polyamorous
NYC

1

2

3

SanteCoffee

Invictus

American HeartWalk
MARCH 6, 2003

4

DREAM CARS

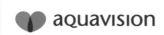

aquavision

5

	A	**B**	**C**	**D**
1		 COLLIERVILLE UNITED METHODIST CHURCH		  TORRID ROMANCE
2			CEASE FIRE SPRINKLER COMPANY, LLC	BALLET WICHITA DANCE EXPERIENCE
3				PARAHAMSA
4		INDOMITABLE SPIRIT 不動心		FIREHOUSE LOUNGE
5				

1

2

3

4

5

D = Design Firm   **C** = Client

	A	B	C	D
1	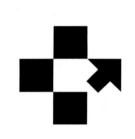			
2				
3	 			
4				
5				

Newslink
Identity Design

Hat-trick Design Consultants, London, United Kingdom

The success of Newslink's logo has as much to do with its initial design as it does with its consistent and effective implementation in direct mail, says Hat-trick Design art director Gareth Howat.

Newslink is a media product in the United Kingdom that allows radio advertisers to buy air immediate before and after newscasts, a period that elicits the highest levels of listener attention during the broadcast day. It is a premium product, somewhat costly, but very effective, says Howat.

Media buyers who might consider purchasing Newslink space are typically inundated with other buy options and promotions. So Newslink had to stand out in a simple and clear way in order to cut through the clutter.

"Media buyers get so much direct mail, a logo can only do so much to attract attention. Newslink's mailers and online environment, together with the logo, would be important in getting across key messages," the designer explains.

Howat began by exploring the notion of people who are listening, of sound waves, and of digital level bars that might be seen on sound control equipment. The client immediately embraced a concept in which the word *in,* already embedded in the name Newslink, was highlighted with color and brackets. Not only did the brackets frame the word *in,* they also resembled sound waves.

Framing *in* had another benefit: With expressions such as *in mind, in tune, in reach,* and *in depth,* the logo could be turned into its own changeable tagline.

"It's a flexible logo that we can change over time," Howat says of the mark, which today has five permutations. "It allows us to verbally pull out the core values of the product." The brackets device was also used to highlight other pieces of copy on key applications.

But Howat believes the direct mail Hat-trick created for Newslink made the logo come to life. The designs have a clean, visual style. The simpler and more direct, the better, he believes.

For example, Hat-trick created a card, printed in red and green, that was sent out with a red plastic filter that filtered out the red, cluttered text, representative of the overwhelming media noise that Newslink cuts out. The proof of the firm's approach was in the reaction of the mailer's approximately 5,000 recipients; it achieved an admirable 4.2 percent response where 0.5 percent is considered normal.

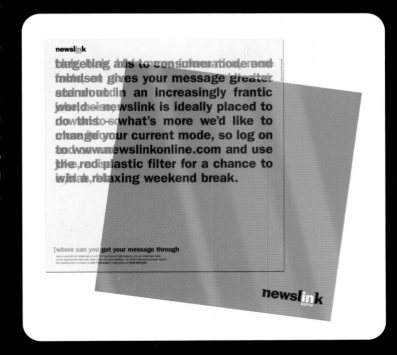

	A	B	C	D

LOGO SEARCH

Keywords [**Arts**]

Type: ○ Symbol ○ Typographic ○ Combo ● All

snapshots

SHORT END PRODUCTIONS, LLC

picturebrains

laughing stock

STIPHOUT
photo & styling

CHRIS KELLY
PRODUCTIONS

DENNIS FAGAN STUDIOS
STILL AND MOVING PICTURES

cinego

ORGANIC FILMS

TVbyGirls

TV by GIRLS

1C Ⓓ Chimera Design Ⓒ Smart Shots 1D Ⓓ The Oesterle Ⓒ Freisteller

2A Ⓓ zengigi design Ⓒ Christina Maxwell 2B Ⓓ CONCEPTiCONS Ⓒ Lorin Crosby 2C Ⓓ Hallmark Cards Inc. Ⓒ Hallmark Cards, Inc. 2D Ⓓ Idle Hands Design Ⓒ Short End Productions, LLC

3A Ⓓ o2 ideas Ⓒ Picture Brains 3B Ⓓ Steve's Portfolio Ⓒ Laughing Stock 3C Ⓓ Straka Dusan Ⓒ Stiphout 3D Ⓓ ykcreative, LLC Ⓒ Chris Kelly

4A Ⓓ Edward Allen Ⓒ Dennis Fagan 4B Ⓓ The Oesterle Ⓒ Christoph Kappl 4C Ⓓ The Oesterle Ⓒ Cinema 4D Ⓓ Jonathan Rice & Company Ⓒ RadioShack

5A Ⓓ Creative Kong Ⓒ Organic Films 5B Ⓓ Werner Design Werks Ⓒ TVbyGirls 5C Ⓓ Werner Design Werks Ⓒ TVbyGirls 5D Ⓓ Les Kerr Creative Ⓒ The Station Store

	A	B	C	D
1				
2				
3				
4				
5				

Ⓓ = Design Firm   Ⓒ = Client

1A Ⓓ Rome & Gold Creative Ⓒ World-View Café   1B Ⓓ Fernandez Design Ⓒ Citrix   1C Ⓓ The Oesterle Ⓒ Micro Consult   1D Ⓓ Glitschka Studios Ⓒ Glitschka Studios

2A Ⓓ HMK Archive Ⓒ NPR KSTX   2B Ⓓ Fuego3 Ⓒ Weapon Records   2C Ⓓ delit-k-delice Ⓒ urban records   2D Ⓓ MEME ENGINE Ⓒ ANYISM   3A Ⓓ IMAGWHAUS Ⓒ University of Minnesota

3B Ⓓ Carbone Smolan Agency Ⓒ Chicago Symphony Orchestra   3C Ⓓ Whaley Design, Ltd Ⓒ Withrow Ballroom, Katrina Relief Concert   3D Ⓓ Savage Synapses Unltd. Ⓒ Wyclef Jean/Yclef Records

4A Ⓓ Sommese Design Ⓒ Penn State Jazz Club   4B Ⓓ Associated Advertising Agency, Inc. Ⓒ KACY Radio   4C Ⓓ Associated Advertising Agency, Inc. Ⓒ KACY Radio   4D Ⓓ Fox Parlor Ⓒ Wendy Tremont king

5A Ⓓ Blacktop Creative Ⓒ American Jazz Museum   5B Ⓓ Glitschka Studios Ⓒ Brian Carlson Drumming   5C Ⓓ Werner Design Werks Ⓒ VH1   5D Ⓓ Monster Design Company Ⓒ Benicia Performing Arts Foundation

	A	B	C	D
1				
2				
3				
4				
5				

Ⓓ = Design Firm   Ⓒ = Client

1A Ⓓ Werner Design Werks Ⓒ Werner Design Werks Inc. 1B Ⓓ Gardner Design Ⓒ Russell Public Relations 1C Ⓓ Henjum Creative Ⓒ Language Links 1D Ⓓ Banowetz + Company, Inc. Ⓒ GLAAD

2A Ⓓ FUSZION Collaborative Ⓒ CADCA 2B Ⓓ Strange Ideas Ⓒ bad idea 2C Ⓓ HRM Ⓒ John E. H. Butler 2D Ⓓ Steven O'Connor Ⓒ Cyphon Design

3A Ⓓ Little Jacket Ⓒ Local Girl Gallery 3B Ⓓ Owen Design Ⓒ Principal 3C Ⓓ Jon Flaming Design Ⓒ Helen Houp 3D Ⓓ Bronson Ma Creative Ⓒ Deep Ellum

4A Ⓓ Davies Associates Ⓒ Cox Paint 4B Ⓓ Crackerbox Ⓒ Gigi Hair Salon 4C Ⓓ Tunglid Advertising Agency ehf. Ⓒ Haircastle 4D Ⓓ Banowetz + Company, Inc. Ⓒ Dean Banowetz

5A Ⓓ Gardner Design Ⓒ A&M Upholstery 5B Ⓓ ComGroup Ⓒ Kevin Rowley 5C Ⓓ Rule29 Ⓒ Rockport Publishers 5D Ⓓ Idle Hands Design Ⓒ (student project)

LOGO SEARCH

Keywords **Miscellaneous**

Type: ○ Symbol ○ Typographic ○ Combo ● All

 dataTrust

1

ROMANO®

DAVIDSON ENTERPRISES

A T L A S
B O O K S

ALLWOOD

DINABEAN

2

DRUM
DF
FOUNDRY

CLAIM
S
TO FAME

BELISLE
C O N S T R U C T I O N

3

Bad
IDEAS

TCP

SEXICIDE
FLAMMABLE

4

SEARCH

DUO
COMMUNICATIONS
the power of two

5

	A	**B**	**C**	**D**
1				
2				
3				
4				
5				

Ⓓ = Design Firm　　Ⓒ = Client

1A Ⓓ MINE Ⓒ Brainfloss　1B Ⓓ Gardner Design Ⓒ Material Comforts　1C Ⓓ Glitschka Studios Ⓒ Christ's Church　1D Ⓓ Pix Design, inc. Ⓒ The Woods

2A Ⓓ Dotzero Design Ⓒ Boise Paper　2B Ⓓ Les Kerr Creative Ⓒ Wickliffe Land & Cattle Co.　2C Ⓓ Thielen Designs Ⓒ Hyperactive Music Magazine　2D Ⓓ www.iseedots.com Ⓒ Government Executive

3A Ⓓ Archrival Ⓒ Jim Esch for U.S. Congress　3B Ⓓ Type G Ⓒ Road Runner Sports　3C Ⓓ ellen bruss design Ⓒ Moxie　3D Ⓓ rehab(r) communications graphics Ⓒ A Little Black Dress

4A Ⓓ Ammunition Ⓒ The Mad Group Ltd　4B Ⓓ Studio Arts and Letters Ⓒ luckybar　4C Ⓓ Deuce Creative Ⓒ Deuce Creative (self-promotion)　4D Ⓓ Edward Allen Ⓒ Hyena Editorial

5A Ⓓ Studio Simon Ⓒ Corpus Christi Hooks　5B Ⓓ IMAGEHAUS Ⓒ Far Fetched Spirits　5C Ⓓ dandy idea Ⓒ DogBoy's Dog Ranch　5D Ⓓ Funk/Levis & Associates, Inc. Ⓒ WetDawg

A	B	C	D	

LOGO SEARCH

Keywords **Food**

Type: ○ Symbol ○ Typographic ○ Combo ● All

1

2

3

4

5

 = Design Firm    = Client

1C Ⓓ Grapefruit Ⓒ Language of the Leaf   1D Ⓓ Strange Ideas Ⓒ Riverside Coffee

2A Ⓓ Strange Ideas Ⓒ coffee icon   2B Ⓓ Strange Ideas Ⓒ cubist coffee   2C Ⓓ Bryan Cooper Design Ⓒ Gold Coast Gourmet Market   2D Ⓓ Visual Inventro Ltd. Co. Ⓒ Fitzgerald Assoc./Brunswick Bowling

3A Ⓓ Blue Tricycle, Inc. Ⓒ Connect Café, Inc.   3B Ⓓ Barnstorm Creative Group Inc. Ⓒ Wicked Café   3C Ⓓ Elephant In The Room Ⓒ Glass Half Full   3D Ⓓ R&D Thinktank Ⓒ Domaine Haleaux

4A Ⓓ Strange Ideas Ⓒ escape plan   4B Ⓓ A3 Design Ⓒ Valley Winery   4C Ⓓ Rick Johnson & Company Ⓒ Sigs   4D Ⓓ Edward Allen Ⓒ Key Bar

5A Ⓓ Rick Johnson & Company Ⓒ OilSlick Imports   5B Ⓓ Insight Design Ⓒ My Volunteer Center   5C Ⓓ Brand Engine Ⓒ SkylarHaley   5D Ⓓ Werner Design Werks Ⓒ Simple Simon

171

	A	B	C	D
1				
2				
3				
4				
5				

	A	B	C	D	
1					1
2					2
3					3
4					4
5					5

A – **B** – **C** – **D**

🄳 = Design Firm   🄲 = Client

Emory University
Identity Design

Joe Bosack Graphic Design Company, Pipersville, Pennsylvania

Joe Bosack Graphic Design Company is one of handful of design firms that specialize in sports branding. It's an endlessly interesting field, Joe Bosack says, but one of its main pitfalls is that the majority of his office's designs are redesigns of logos with which fans have longstanding and emotional relationships.

"People are passionate about their sports teams. A team's logo directly represents those passions, and when you start to mess with it, especially at the collegiate level, fans can get upset," he says.

That's why the logo Bosack created for the Emory Eagles of Emory University was a refreshing change of pace: No one had any allegiance whatsoever to the athletic department's old logo—essentially a clip art eagle that looked like it had a bad headache.

The project presented unique challenges. Emory University is best known for academics, although some of its athletic teams are national contenders. Its tennis team is a national champion. Trouble is, tennis is not a sport that brings rabid fans out in droves. And the school does not have a football team at all.

In discussions with his client, Bosack discovered that the athletic department wanted a logo that was strong but not overly aggressive or mean-looking, as many college athletic mascot logos are. No exposed, flared talons, he says. The goal was to develop an identity that fit within the overall perception of Emory.

This is a well-respected, elite institution, and the identity we developed reinforces that perception."

He began his work by considering Emory University's logo, a new design that was the outcome of a recent institutional rebranding. The new logo featured a shield shape, and Bosack thought this held promise as an effective connector to athletics.

Another element he found interesting was the letter E. As he explored its shape, he came upon numerous ways to transform the letterform into an eagle or part of an eagle. In the end, the favorite design of the ten Bosack presented was an impassive eagle, its head serving alone as the centerpiece of a shield or as the crossbar on an E.

Almost as important as the logo in sports branding are the colors that are selected, Bosack explains. Emory's school colors are royal blue and a bright gold—not fashionable or "wearable" colors, he felt. Outside of athletic uniforms, in fact, the colors were rarely seen on campus. So Bosack toned the scheme down to a navy blue and a mustard yellow.

The more muted system also helped make accurate reproduction easier to achieve: Many unrelated vendors must be relied on to furnish branded products. "We have to consider what will be practical when the client translates work to the practical world, whether that's through uniforms or decals or whatever," he says.

(Below) Original design

LOGO SEARCH

Keywords **Structures**

Type: ○ Symbol ○ Typographic ○ Combo ● All

1

HousingWorks
AUSTIN

home **partners**

2

THE JOY SCHOOL
UNLOCKING A CHILD'S LEARNING POTENTIAL

3

eTRUST

HARIE
Housing & Redevelopment Insurance Exchange

firehouse
LOUNGE

4

OSD

ISGRIG | *mortgage* | GROUP

HOME FAIR

5

	A	B	C	D
1				
2				
3				
4				
5				

Ⓓ = Design Firm   Ⓒ = Client

A	B	C	D

 A   **B**   **C**   **D**

   **1**

    **2**

    **3**

    **4**

    **5**

D = Design Firm   **C** = Client

	A	B	C	D
1				
2				
3				
4				
5				

1A Ⓓ GSD&M Ⓒ Alamo Hotels   1B Ⓓ Hubbell Design Works Ⓒ Fireball Bowling   1C Ⓓ Werner Design Werks Ⓒ Archer Farms for Target   1D Ⓓ Gee + Chung Design Ⓒ Sun Microsystems   2A Ⓓ Maycreate Ⓒ Whitehall Properties

2B Ⓓ Whitney Edwards LLC Ⓒ Eastern Shore Title Company   2C Ⓓ GSD&M Ⓒ City of Austin   2D Ⓓ Bemporad Baranowski Marketing Group Ⓒ Robert Wood Johnson Health Policy Fellowships Program

3A Ⓓ Corduroy Ⓒ Tandem Marketing   3B Ⓓ maximo, inc. Ⓒ Frontera de Ceramica   3C Ⓓ Werner Design Werks Ⓒ Textbooks.com   3D Ⓓ Owen Design Ⓒ Inner Flora

4A Ⓓ David Russell Design Ⓒ Mucci Trucksess Architecture and Interiors   4B Ⓓ Ramp Ⓒ Mark Steward Securities   4C Ⓓ www.iseedots.com Ⓒ Vertex Studios   4D Ⓓ nicelogo.com Ⓒ Clegg

5A Ⓓ Strategy Studio Ⓒ Tucker Anthony Sutro   5B Ⓓ Axiom Design Group Ⓒ Yokahama University   5C Ⓓ Dashwood Design Ltd Ⓒ Rubicon   5D Ⓓ CAPSULE Ⓒ CapsuleShak

LOGO SEARCH

Keywords **Transportation**

Type: ○ Symbol ○ Typographic ○ Combo ● All

SOULAR

Propulsion Media, Inc.

BestNotes.com
his notes, her thoughts, your grade

ascentives
corporate speciality solutions

	A	B	C	D
1				
2				
3				
4				
5				

Ⓓ = Design Firm   Ⓒ = Client

1A Ⓓ Jon Flaming Design Ⓒ Red Cab Design   1B Ⓓ Fresh Oil Ⓒ AudioStop   1C Ⓓ Felixsockwell.com Ⓒ goodwill   1D Ⓓ Sterling Brands Ⓒ Artwagen

2A Ⓓ judson design associates Ⓒ glasswall Restaurant   2B Ⓓ sheean design Ⓒ Unfiltered Napa   2C Ⓓ Ross Creative + Strategy Ⓒ We Care Transport   2D Ⓓ Sockeye Creative Ⓒ Red Truck Publishing

3A Ⓓ GSD&M Ⓒ Trout Trucking   3B Ⓓ TBF Creative Ⓒ Bak-A-Bush Adventures   3C Ⓓ Reynolds + Associates Ⓒ Indianapolis Police Motorcycle Drill Team   3D Ⓓ Matt Whitley Ⓒ Indy Motor Speedway

4A Ⓓ Brainding Ⓒ Motorcycle   4B Ⓓ R&R Partners Ⓒ Moto Logo   4C Ⓓ R&R Partners Ⓒ Throttle 2   4D Ⓓ Motorcycle Safety Foundation Ⓒ Scooter School

5A Ⓓ David Kampa Ⓒ Texas Bicycle Coalition   5B Ⓓ Greg Walters Design Ⓒ BreakAway Consulting   5C Ⓓ Sandstrom Design Ⓒ adidas   5D Ⓓ Strange Ideas Ⓒ shark racing

1

2

3

4

5

D = Design Firm   **C** = Client

1A **D** Howling Good Designs **C** Spokeswomen Cycling Team   1B **D** Studio GT&P **C** Tessuti di Montefalco Srl   1C **D** octane inc. **C** Carolina Heritage Line   1D **D** Miles Design **C** Java Train

2A **D** Praxis Studios **C** Five Star Restaurant   2B **D** Formikula **C** Die Artillerie   2C **D** octane inc. **C** JB Communications   2D **D** FUSZION Collaborative **C** Atlantis Events

3A **D** Eisenberg and Associates **C** Seven Ships   3B **D** Sandstrom Design **C** Full Sail   3C **D** Bryan Cooper Design **C** The Center for the Physically Challenged   3D **D** Nick Glenn Design **C** Seven Seafood Bar and Grill

4A **D** Gardner Design **C** Navential   4B **D** Gee + Chung Design **C** Castile Ventures   4C **D** Ramp **C** Viking Star Enterprises   4D **D** Stephan and Herr **C** AMP Incorporated

5A **D** Fresh Oil **C** 22 Bowen's Wine Bar & Grille   5B **D** Sabingrafik, Inc. **C** Sempra Energy   5C **D** Harkey Design **C** Snug Harbour   5D **D** northfound **C** Catering St. Louis

index

directory

(twentystar)
United States
303.596.4134
www.twentystar.com

1 Trick Pony
United States
646.485.8831
www.1trickpony.com

28 LIMITED BRAND
Germany
49.20.939.4238
www.mircommedia.de

2cdesign
United States
214.599.9078
www.2cdesign.com

343 Creative
United States
718.720.7779
www.343creative.com

38one
United Kingdom
44.79.6823.8671
www.38one.com

4sight Communication
United States
323.954.3550
www.get4sight.com

68Design
United States
404.861.5756
www.68design.com

9fps
United States
312.697.1530
www.9fps.net

9MYLES, Inc.
United States
858.344.8619
www.9myles.com

A3 Design
United States
704.568.5351
www.athreedesign.com

Actual Size Creative
United States
412.421.3279
www.thisisactualsize.com

adbass:designs LLC
United States
516.285.0385
www.adbassdesigns.com

Addison Whitney
United States
704.347.5700
www.addisonwhitney.com

AKOFA Creative
United States
404.915.8127
www.akofa.com

Alesce
United States
303.229.8100
www.alesce.com

Ali Cindoruk
United States
212.673.5517
www.alicindoruk.com

Allen Creative
United States
770.972.8862
www.allencreative.com

Alphabet Arm Design
United States
617.451.9990
www.alphabetarmdesign.com

America Online
United States
614.538.4632
www.netscape.com

Ammunition
United Kingdom
44.207.241.2233
www.ammunition.uk

amyHELLER design
United States
203.773.1988
www.amyhellerdesign.com

angryporcupine*design
United States
435.655.0645
www.angryporcupine.com

Anoroc
United States
919.821.1191
www.anorocagency.com

Archrival
United States
402.435.2525
www.archrival.com

Ardoise Design
Canada
514.287.1002
www.ardoise.com

Armeilia Subianto Design
Indonesia
62.21.527.4364
www.asubiantodesign.com

Armstrong International CI
China
86.10.8472.0531
www.AICI.cn

ArtGraphics.ru
Russia
7.095.730.5233
www.artgraphics.ru

ASGARD
Russia
7.812.389.0631
www.asgard-design.com

Associated Advertising Agency, Inc.
United States
316.683.4691
www.associatedadv.com

Atha Design
United States
641.673.2820

Aurora Design
United States
518.346.6228
www.auroradesignonline.com

Axiom Design Group
United States
713.523.5711
www.axiomdg.com

Axiom Design Partners
Western Australia
61.8.9381.6270
www.axiomdp.com.au

B.L.A. Design Company
United States
803.518.4130

b5 Marketing & Kommunikation GmbH
Germany
49.06201.8790731
www.b5-media.de

baba designs
United States
248.360.1251
www.anniewidmyer.com

Bakken Creative Co.
United States
510.540.8260
www.bakkencreativeco.com

Banowetz + Company, Inc.
United States
214.823.7300
www.banowetz.com

Barnstorm Creative
United States
719.630.7200
www.barnstormcreative.biz

Barnstorm Creative Group Inc.
Canada
604.681.3377
www.barnstormcreative.com

batesneimand inc.
United States
202.637.9732
www.batesneimand.com

BCM/D
United States
410.290.5290

Bemporad Baranowski Marketing Group
United States
212.473.4902
www.bbmg.com

Big Bald Guy Design Studio
United States
303.843.9777
www.envision-grp.com

Blacktop Creative
United States
816.221.1585
www.blacktopcreative.com

Blattner Brunner
United States
412.995.9585
www.blattnerbrunner.com

BLOOM LLC
United States
415.451.1866
www.bloommedia.com

Blue Storm Design
New Zealand
64.4.562.8771
www.bluestormdesign.co.nz

Blue Studios, Inc.
United States
410.342.3600
www.bluestudios.com

Blue Tricycle, Inc.
United States
612.729.2372
www.bluetricycle.com

Boelts/Stratford Associates
United States
520.792.1026
www.boeltsstratford.com

Bonilla Design
United States
847.791.3491

Boom Creative
United States
216.291.2411
www.boom-creative.com

Born to Design
United States
317.838.9404
www.born-to-design.com

Brady Design Ltd.
United States
614.299.6661
www.bradydesignltd.com

Brainding
Argentina
www.brainding.com.ar

Brand Bird
United States
404.373.2950
www.brandbird.com

Brand Engine
United States
415.339.4220
www.brandengine.com

Brand Navigation
United States
541.549.4425
www.brandnavigation.com

Brandesign
United States
609.490.9700
www.brandesign.com

Brandia
Portugal
351.213.923000
www.brandia.net

Brandient
Romania
40.21.222.8167
www.brandient.com

BrandSavvy, Inc.
United States
303.471.9991
www.brandsavvyinc.com

Braue; Branding & Corporate Design
Germany
49.471.983820
www.braue.info

Brian Blankenship
United States
817.917.8379
www.brianblankenship.com

Brian Collins Design
United States
417.890.5933
www.williamscollins.com

Brian Sooy & Co.
United States
440.322.5142
www.briansooy.com

Bright Strategic Design
United States
310.305.2565
www.brightdesign.com

Bristol-Myers Squibb Company
United States
609.897.3143
www.bms.com

Bronson Ma Creative
United States
214.457.5615
www.bronsonma.com

Brook Group, LTD
United States
410.465.7805
www.brookgroup.com

Bryan Cooper Design
United States
918.732.3333
www.bryancooperdesign.com
www.cooperillustration.com

Bull's-Eye Creative Communications
United States
404.352.3006
www.bullseyecreative
communications.com

Bunch
Croatia
385.14.920855
www.bunchdesign.com

C. Cady Design
United States
423.843.0456
www.ccadydesign.com

Campbell Fisher Design
United States
602.955.2707
www.thinkcfd.com

CAPSULE
United States
612.341.4525
www.capsule.us

Carbone Smolan Agency
United States
212.807.0011
www.carbonsmolan.com

Carol Gravelle Graphic Design
United States
805.383.2773
www.carolgravelledesign.com

Catch Design Studio
United States
206.322.4323
www.catchstudio.com

Cato Purnell Partners
Australia
61.3.9429.6577
www.catopartners.com

cc design
United States
423.926.3737

CDI Studios
United States
702.876.3316
www.cdistudios.com

Cfx
United States
314.968.1161
www.cfx-inc.com

CH & LER Design
United States
801.966.9171

Chad Carr Design/Westcarr
United States
612.331.4350
www.westcarr.com

Cheri Gearhart, graphic design
United States
708.34634855
www.gearhartdesign.com

Chimera Design
Australia
61.3.9593.6844
www.chimera.com.au

Chris Malven Design
United States
515.450.9023
www.chrismalven.com

christiansen: creative
United States
715.381.8480
www.christiansencreative.com

Church Logo Gallery
United States
760.231.9368
www.churchlogogallery.com

Cisneros Design
United States
505.471.6699
www.cisnerosdesign.com

Clark Studios
United States
949.351.5925
www.clark-studios.com

Coleman Creative
United States
832.797.1682

Colle + McVoy
United States
952.852.7500
www.collemcvoy.com

ComGroup
United States
404.892.4474
www.comgroupmra.com

Communique Group
United States
303.220.5080
www.thecommuniquegroup.com

CONCEPTiCONS
United States
818.259.2725
www.concepticons.com

concussion, llc
United States
817.336.6824
www.concussion.net

Corduroy
United States
214.827.3007
www.corduroydesign.com

Corporate Express
United States
303.664.2000
www.CorporateExpress.com

Cotterteam
United States
410.276.3794
www.nitrobranddesign.com

Crackerbox
United States
617.437.7549
www.crackerbox.us

Creative Kong
United States
512.589.6160
www.creativekong.com

Crescent Lodge
United Kingdom
44.0.20.7613.0613
www.crescentlodge.co.uk

CS Design
United States
320.493.5854

Curtis Sayers Design
United States
617.947.2720
www.csayersdesign.com

Curtis Sharp Design
United States
206.366.7975
www.curtissharpdesign.com

d4 creative group
United States
215.483.4555
www.d4creative.com

dale harris
Australia
41.189.9840
www.daleharris.com

Dan Rood Design
United States
785.842.4870
www.danrooddesign.com

dandy idea
United States
512.627.9103
www.dandyidea.com

Dashwood Design Ltd
New Zealand
64.9307.0901
www.dashwooddesign.com.nz

David Kampa
United States
512.636.3791
www.kampadesign.com

David Maloney Design
United States
612.396.2548
www.david-maloney.com

David Russell Design
United States
206.621.1360
www.davidrusselldesign.com

Davies Associates
United States
310.247.9572
www.daviesla.com

davpunk!
United States
847.345.7865
www.davpunk.com

Day Six Creative
United States
972.548.7337
www.daysixcreative.com

DDB
United States
312.552.6124
www.ddb.com

DDB Dallas
United States
214.259.4200
www.ddbdallas.com

dedstudios
United States
310.850.2161

Deep Design
United States
404.266.7500
www.deepdesign.com

Delikatessen
Germany
49.40.350.8060
www.delikatessen-hamburg.com

delit-k-delice
France
33.1.499.771.984
www.absolutely-design.com

Desgrippes Gobé
United States
212.979.8900
www.dga.com

Design and Image
United States
303.292.3455
www.designandimage.com

Design MG/DMG
Panama
507.214.1781.1700

Design Nut
United States
301.942.2360
www.designnut.com

Design One
United States
828.254.7898
www.d1inc.com

designlab, inc
United States
314.962.7702
www.designlabinc.com

Designsensory
United States
865.690.2249
www.designsensory.com

design-studio Muhina
Russia
7.3412.76.3315
www.muhina.com

Deuce Creative
United States
713.863.8633
www.deucecreative.com

Diagram
Poland
48.61.664.8081
www.diagram.pl

Dialekt Design
Canada
450.226.1440
www.dialektdesign.com

**DIRECT DESIGN
Visual Branding**
Russia
7.095.916.01.23
www.directdesign.ru

Dirty Design
United Kingdom
44.0.117.927.3344
www.dirtydesign.co.uk

Ditto!
United States
914.478.3641
www.dittodoesit.com

dmayne design
United States
417.823.8058
www.dmaynedesign.com

Doink, Inc.
United States
305.529.0121
www.doinkdesign.com

Dotfive
United States
415.354.1076
www.dotfive.com

Dotzero Design
United States
503.892.9262
www.DotzeroDesign.com

Doug Beatty
Canada
416.826.3684
www.taxizone.com

Dr. Alderete
Mexico
52.55.1998.4688
www.jorgealderete.com

Dreamedia Studios
United States
501.954.9711
www.dreamediastudios.com

Duffy & Partners
United States
612.548.2333
www.duffy.com

Eben Design
United States
206.523.9010
www.ebendesign.com

Edward Allen
United States
512.443.2102

eindruck design
United States
406.829.1581
www.eindruckdesign.com

Eisenberg and Associates
United States
214.528.5990
www.eisenberg-inc.com

Elaine Park
United States
312.384.1906
www.commongroundmktg.com

Element
United States
614.447.0906
www.elementville.com

Elephant in the Room
United States
336.624.9844
www.elephantintheroom.biz

Eleven Feet Media
United States
650.278.2451
www.elevenfeetmedia.com

elf design
United States
650.358.9973
www.elf-design.com

ellen bruss design
United States
303.830.8323
www.ebd.com

emblem
Venezuela
58.212.243.2969
www.mblm.com

Emphasize LLC
United States
718.932.7810
www.mariavilla.com

Entermotion Design Studio
United States
316.264.2277
www.entermotion.com

Enterprise
South Africa
27.11.319.8000
www.enterpriseig.co.zg

Eric Baker Design Assoc., Inc.
United States
212.598.9111
www.ericbakerdesign.com

Exti Dzyn
United States
818.679.9116
www.extidzyn.com

Eyebeam Creative LLC
United States
202.518.5888
www.eyebeamcreative.com

Eyescape
United Kingdom
44.0.20.8521.0342
www.eyescape.co.uk

fallindesign studio
Russia
7.812.461.1985
www.faldin.ru

Farah Design, Inc.
United States
786.267.2954
www.farahdesign.com &
www.visiom.com

Farm Design
United States
310.828.1624
www.farmdesign.net

Fauxkoi
United States
612.251.4277
www.fauxkoi.com

Felixsockwell.com
United States
917.657.8880
www.felixsockwell.com

Fernandez Design
United States
512.619.4020
www.fernandezdesign.com

Fifth Letter
United States
336.723.5655
www.fifth-letter.com

FigDesign
United States
972.259.5900
www.figdesign.com

FiveStone
United States
678.730.0686
www.fivestone.com

Flaxenfield, Inc.
United States
336.218.0530
www.flaxenfield.com

Floor 84 Studio
United States
818.754.1231
www.floor84studio.com

Formikula
Germany
49.0.89.48.00.45.64
www.marc-herold.com

Fox Parlor
United States
415.734.9450
www.foxparlor.com

Franke+Fiorella
United States
612.338.1700
www.frankefiorella.com

Fredrik Lewander
Sweden
46.73.955.9968
www.fredriklewander.se

Fresh Oil
United States
401.709.4656
www.freshoil.com

Freshwater Design
United States
678.910.6381
www.freshwaterdesign.net

Fuego3
United States
817.937.1605
www.fuego3.com

Funk/Levis & Associates, Inc.
United States
541.485.1932
www.funklevis.com

FUSZION Collaborative
United States
703.548.8080
www.fuszion.com

FutureBrand
United States
212.931.6300
www.futurebrand.com

FutureBrand Melbourne
Australia
61.3.9604.2777
www.futurebrand.com

FutureBrand Buenos Aires
Argentina
54.11.4777.2277
www.futurebrand.com

Fuze
United States
775.626.4577
www.ifuze.com

FWIS
United States
503.230.1741
www.fwis.com

Gabi Toth
Romania
4.072.253.3715
www.toth.ro

Gabriel Kalach *
V I S U A L communications
United States
305.532.2336

Gabriela Gasparini Design
United States
718.417.1064
www.gabrielagasparini.com

Gardner Design
United States
316.691.8808
www.gardnerdesign.com

Garfinkel Design
United States
706.369.6831
www.garfinkeldesign.com

Gee + Chung Design
United States
415.543.1192
www.geechungdesign.com

Gee Creative
United States
843.853.3086
www.geecreative.com

GetElevatedDesign.com
United States
www.ejhartley.com

**ginger griffin marketing
and design**
United States
704.896.2479
www.wehaveideas.com

GingerBee Creative
United States
406.443.3032
www.gingerbee.com

Glitschka Studios
United States
971.223.6143
www.vonglitschka.com

Goldforest
United States
305.573.7370
www.goldforest.com

GRAF d'SIGN creative boutique
Russia
7.916.686.2812
www.gdscb.com

GrafiQa Graphic Design
United States
607.433.8837
www.grafiqa.com

Grapefruit
Romania
40.232.233.066

Greg Walters Design
United States
206.362.1310

greteman group
United States
316.263.1004
www.gretemangroup.com

Gridwerk
United States
215.872.6266
www.gridwerk.net

GSCS
United Arab Emirates
971.4391.0873
www.greggsedgwick.com

GSD&M
United States
512.242.4602
www.gsdm.com

Haley Johnson Design
United States
612.722.8050
haley@hja.com

Hallmark Cards Inc.
United States
816.545.6753
www.hallmark.com

Hammerpress
United States
816.421.1929
www.hammerpress.net

Hanna & Associates
United States
208.661.9455
www.cdaoriginals.com

HardBall Sports
United States
904.998.8778
www.hardballcreative.com

Harkey Design
United States
404.609.9090
www.harkeydesign.com

Harwood Kirsten Leigh McCoy
South Africa
27.83.441.0174
www.hklm.co.za

Hat-trick Design Consultants
United Kingdom
44.0.20.7403.7875
www.hat-trickdesign.co.uk

Hausch Design Agency LLC
United States
414.628.3976
www.hauschdesign.com

Hayes + Company
Canada
416.536.5438
www.hayesandcompany.com

Henjum Creative
United States
920.866.3738

Hill Design Studios
United States
503.507.1228
www.hilldesignstudios.com

Hinge
United States
703.391.8870
www.pivotalbrands.com

**Hipflix.com/The 5659
Design Co.**
United States
773.685.7019
www.hipflix.com

**Hirshorn Zuckerman
Design Group**
United States
301.294.6302

HMK Archive
United States
210.473.1961
www.sharkthang.com

Honey Design
Canada
519.679.0786
www.honey.on.ca

Hope Advertising
Australia
61.3.9529.7799
www.hope.com.au

Hornall Anderson
United States
206.826.2329
www.hadw.com

Howerton + White Interactive
United States
316.262.6644
www.howertonwhite.com

Howling Good Designs
United States
631.427.4769
www.howlinggooddesigns.com

Hoyne Design
Australia
61.39.537.1822
www.hoyne.com.au

HRM
United States
985.879.2443
www.hrmcreative.com

Hubbell Design Works
United States
714.227.3457
www.hubbelldesignworks.com

HuebnerPetersen
United States
970.663.9344

humanot
United States
716.604.4026
www.humanot.com

Hutchinson Associates, Inc.
United States
312.455.9191
www.hutchinson.com

i3design
United States
610.828.6442
www.i3design.us

i4 Solutions
United States
801.294.6400
www.i4.net

Idea Girl Design
United States
310.623.2288
www.ideagirldesign.com

idGO Advertising
United States
401.368.1049

Idle Hands Design
United States
917.690.2383
www.idlehandsnyc.com

Ikola designs
United States
763.533.3440

IMA Design, Corp.
Russia
7.095.262.5985
www.Imadesign.ru

IMAGEHAUS
United States
612.377.8700
www.imagehaus.net

Imaginaria
United States
214.257.8704
www.imaginariacreative.com

INNFUSION Studios
United States
800.996.7616
www.innfusionstudios.com

Insight Design
United States
316.262.0085

Insomniac Creative Studio
United States
www.insomniaccs.com

Integer Group - Midwest
United States
515.288.7910
www.interger.com

**Interrobang Design
Collaborative, Inc.**
United States
802.434.5970
www.interrobangdesign.com

Intersection Creative
United States
602.622.8757
www.intersectioncreative.com

Iperdesign, Inc.
United States
917.412.9045
www.iperdesign.com

ivan2design
United States
206.364.8996
www.ivan2.com

j6Studios
www.j6studios.com

**Jason Kirshenblatt/
The O Group**
United States
212.398.0100
www.ogroup.net

Jason Pillon
United States
925.243.1936

**JC Thomas Marketing/
Advertising**
United States
704.377.9660
www.thoughtville.com

Jeff Pollard Design
United States
503.246.7251
www.jpd-logos.com

Jejak, Rumah Iklan dan Disain
Indonesia
62.21.722.3306
www.jejak.net

Jenny Kolcun Freelance Design
United States
415.331.7202

joe miller's company
United States
408.988.2924

Joi Design
New Zealand
649.377.6684
www.joi.co.nz

Jon Flaming Design
United States
972.235.4880
www.jonflaming.com

Jonathan Rice & Company
United States
817.886.6640
www.jriceco.com

josh higgins design
United States
619.379.2090
www.joshhiggins.com

joven orozco design
United States
949.723.1898
www.jovenville.com

jsDesignCo.
United States
614.353.6412

judson design associates
United States
713.520.1096
www.judsondesign.com

juls design inc
United States
515.963.8309
www.julsdesign.com

Justin Johnson
United States
918.519.1605
www.morebranding.com

Justin Lockwood Design
United States
206.529.7585
www.justinlockwooddesign.com

Kahn Design
United States
760.944.5574
www.kahn-design.com

Kaimere
United Arab Emirates
971.4391.8083
www.tmh.ae

Kendall Creative Shop, Inc.
United States
214.827.6680
www.kendallcreative.com

Kendall Ross
United States
206.262.0540
www.kendallross.com

Kern Design Group
United States
203.329.7070
www.kerndesigngroup.com

Kevin France Design, Inc.
United States
336.765.6213

Keyword Design
United States
219.923.5279
www.keyworddesign.com

Kinesis, Inc.
United States
541.482.3600
www.kinesisinc.com

Kineto
Indonesia
62.21.831.7106
www.kineto.biz

Kitemath
United States
773.252.9908
www.kitemath.com

KOESTER design
United States
469.621.6566
www.koesterdesign.com

KONG Design Group
United States
714.478.9657
www.kongdesigngroup.com

KURT FOR HIRE
United States
917.771.4142
www.kurtforhire.com

KW43 BRANDDESIGN
Germany
49.200.557.7830
www.kw43.gr

Kym Abrams Design
United States
312.654.1005
www.kad.com

label brand
United States
831.421.0518
www.labelbrand.com

**Lance Reed/
tmh the Media House**
United Arab Emirates
971.4391.8083
www.tmh.ae

LandDesign
United States
703.549.7784
www.landdesign.com

Landkamer Partners, Inc.
United States
415.522.2480
www.landkamerpartners.com

Landor Associates
United States
212.614.5261
www.landor.com

Lars Lawson
United States
317.921.0948
www.timberdesignco.com

Lauchpad Creative
United States
405.514.5158
www.launchpad321.com

Leeann Leftwich Zajas Graphic Design
United States
603.702.1044
www.11zdesign.com

Lenox Graphics
United States
401.862.7224
www.lenoxgraphics.com

Les Kerr Creative
United States
972.236.3599
www.leskerr.net

Lesniewicz Associates
United States
419.243.7131
www.designtoinfluence.com

Letter 7
United States
212.595.7445
www.ltr7.com

Lienhart Design
United States
312.738.2200
www.lienhartdesign.com

Lippincott Mercer
United States
212.521.0000
www.lippincottmercer.com

Lisa Speer
United States
917.533.6397
www.lisaspeer.com

Lisa Starace
United States
619.757.6308
www.designactionism.com

Liska + Associates Communication Design
United States
312.644.4400
www.liska.com

Little Jacket
United States
216.373.6979
www.little-jacket.com

Living Creative Design
United States
510.304.0450
www.livingcreative.com

Lizette Gecel
United States
804.359.1711

logobyte design studio
Turkey
90.535.666.6292
www.logobyte.com

LogoDesignSource.com
United States
954.428.8871
www.logodesignsource.com

Lulu Strategy
United States
614.221.3403
www.lulustrategy.com

Lunar Cow
United States
800.594.9620
www.lunarcow.com

Lunar Design
United States
415.252.4388
www.lunar.com

M3 Advertising Design
United States
702.796.6323
www.m3ad.com

Macnab Design Visual Communication
United States
508.286.8558
www.macnabdesign.com

Mad Dog Graphx
United States
907.276.5062
www.thedogpack.com

MANMADE
United States
415.865.9996
www.manmade.com

MannPower Design
United States
973.983.0626
www.mannpowerdesign.com

marc usa
United States
317.632.6501
www.marcusa.com

Maremar Graphic Design
Puerto Rico
787.731.8795
www.maremar.com

Mariqua Design
United States
650.242.4645
www.mariqua.com

markatos
United States
415.235.9203
www.markatos.com

Mary Hutchison Design LLC
United States
206.407.3460
www.maryhutchisondesign.com

Matt Everson Design
United States
608.628.3095
www.matteverson.com

Matt Whitley/Outdoor Cap
United States
479.464.5203
www.outdoorcap.com

mattisimo
United States
415.786.2769
www.mattisimo.com

Mattson Creative
United States
949.388.1772
www.mattsoncreative.com

maximo, inc.
United States
619.269.0063
www.maximoinc.com

Maycreate
United States
423.634.0123
www.maycreate.com

McAndrew Kaps
United States
480.580.5113
www.macandrewkaps.com

mccoycreative
United States
360.920.5260
www.mccoycreative.com

McGuire Design
United States
210.884.4609
www.mcguiredesign.com

McMillian Design
United States
718.636.2097
www.mcmilliandesign.com

MEME ENGINE
United States
212.203.5787
www.memeengine.com

Methodologie
United States
206.623.1044
www.methodologie.com

Metroparks of the Toledo Area
United States
419.407.9735
www.metroparkstoledo.com

Mez Design
United States
715.331.4523
www.mezdesign.com

Miaso Design
United States
773.575.3776
www.miasodesign.com

Michael Courtney Design, Inc.
United States
206.329.8488
www.michaelcourtneydesign.com

Michael Osborne Design
United States
415.255.0125
www.modsf.com

Miles Design
United States
317.915.8693
www.milesdesign.com

Mindgruve
United States
619.757.1325
www.mindgruve.com

Mindspace
United States
480.221.5817
www.mindspaceonline.com

Mindspike Design, LLC
United States
414.765.2344
www.mindspikedesign.com

MINE
United States
415.647.6463
www.minesf.com

Mires/Ball
United States
619.234.6631
www.miresball.com

Miriello Grafico, Inc.
United States
619.234.1124
www.miriellografico.com

Mirko Ilic Corp
United States
212.481.9737
www.mirkoilic.com

Misenheimer Creative, Inc.
United States
770.667.9355
www.misenheimer.com

mixdesign
United States
219.322.7190
www.mixedupworld.com

mk12
United States
816.931.2425
www.mk12.com

Mode Design Studio
United States
214.827.4700
www.modedesignstudio.com

Modern Dog Design Co.
United States
206.789.7667
www.moderndog.com

Mohouse Design Co.
United States
214.321.3193
www.mohousedesign.com

monster design
United States
425.828.7853
www.monsterinvasion.com

Monster Design Company
United States
707.208.5481
www.monsterdesignco.com

Moonsire Design
United States
843.667.3407

Morgan/Mohon
United States
830.990.2888
www.morganmohon.com

morrow mckenzie design
United States
503.222.0331
www.morrowmckenzie.com

Morse and Company Advertising Communication
United States
219.879.1223
www.morseandcompany.com

Moscato Design
United States
630.493.0518

Motorcycle Safety Foundation
United States
949.727.3227
www.msf-usa.org

Motterdesign
Austria
43.5572.3847.0777
www.motter.at

Napoleon design
Brazil
55.11.9935.0300
www.napoleondesign.net

Naughtyfish
Australia
61.2.9327.7942
www.naughtyfish.com

NeoGine Communication Design Ltd.
New Zealand
64.4.385.1792
www.neogine.co.nz

Miles Newlyn/x & y Ltd.
United Kingdom
44.20.7551.4520
contact@newlyn.com

nicelogo.com
United States
949.677.7324
www.nicelogo.com

Nick Glenn Design
United States
281.814.7976
www.nickglenndesign.com

Nita B. Creative
United States
651.644.2889
www.nitabcreative.com

Noble and Associates
United States
417.875.5000
www.noble.net

northfound
United States
215.232.6420
www.northfound.com

Novasoul
United States
818.753.4175
www.novasoul.com

Tom Nynas/R&D Thinktank
United States
214.515.9515
www.randdthinktank.com

Ó!
Iceland
354.562.3300
www.oid.is

o2 ideas
United States
205.949.9494
www.o2ideas.com

oakley design studios
United States
503.241.3705
www.oakleydesign.com

Octane
United States
775.323.7887
www.octanestudios.com

octane inc.
United States
828.693.6699
www.hi-testdesign.com

Octavo Designs
United States
301.695.8885
www.8vodesigns.com

ODM oficina de diseno y marketing
Spain
34.956.265.326
www.odmoficina.com

Off-Leash Studios
United States
617.821.5158
www.offleashstudios.com

Olson + Company
United States
612.215.9800
www.oco.com

OmniStudio Inc.
United States
202.464.3050
www.omnistudio.com

Onoma, LLC
United States
212.253.6570
www.onomadesign.com

Open
United States
212.645.5633
www.notclosed.com

Orange Creative
New Zealand
64.9.273.3688
www.orangecreative.co.nz

Owen Design
United States
515.244.1515
www.chadowendesign.com

Oxide Design Co.
United States
402.344.0168
www.oxidedesign.com

Parachute Design
United States
612.359.4387
www.parachutedesign.com

Paragon Design International
United States
312.832.1030
www.paragondesign
international.com

pat sinclair design
United States
610.896.8616
www.patsinclairdesign.com

Paul Black Design
United States
214.537.9780
www.paulblackdesign.com

Peak Seven Advertising
United States
954.574.0810
www.peakseven.com

Pennebaker
United States
713.963.8607
www.pennebaker.com

Perfect Circle Media Group
United States
972.788.0678
www.perfect360.com

Peters Design
United States
720.348.1053
www.karlpeters.com

Peterson & Company
United States
214.954.0522
www.peterson.com

Phillips Design
United States
813.253.2523
www.portfolios.com/
phillipsdesign

Pix Design, Inc.
United States
212.563.5701
www.pixdesign.com

Pixel Basement
United States
561.376.1899
www.pixelbasement.com

Pixelspace
United States
828.994.2212
www.pixelspace.com

Pixelube
United States
206.216.0278
www.pixelube.com

Playoff Corporation
United States
817.983.0142

pleitezgallo :: design haus
United States
951.961.1524
www.pleitezgallo.com

Polemic Design
United States
201.978.5677
www.polemicdesign.com

Polkadot
Australia
61.1.300.139.398
www.polkadot.com.au

PosterV.Design Studio
Denmark
45.45.85.3575
www.pocs-posters.hv

PowerGroove Creative
United States
720.529.0143

Praxis Studios
United States
919.838.1138
www.praxisstudios.com

Project center
United States
770.979.7684
www.balkecreative.com

Propeller Design
United Arab Emirates
971.4391.4849
www.propeller.ae

proteus
United States
617.263.2211
www.proteusdesign.com

Q
Germany
49.611.181310
www.q-home.de

Quest Fore
United States
412.381.6670
www.questfore.com

R&D Thinktank
United States
214.515.9851
www.randdthinktank.com

R&R Partners
United States
702.318.4360
www.rrpartners.com

rajasandhu.com
Canada
647.668.2547
www.rajasandhu.com

Ramp
United States
213.617.1445
www.rampcreative.com

Red Circle Agency
United States
612.372.4612
www.redcircleagency.com

reduced fat
United States
518.533.9621
www.reduced-fat.com

rehab* communication graphics
United States
206.794.4209
www.rehabgraphics.com

REINES DESIGN INC.
United States
305.373.3181
www.reinesdesign.com

retropup
United States
973.723.5420
www.retropup.com

Reynolds + Associates
United States
310.698.9330
www.372interactive.com

Richards Brock Miller Mitchell & Associates /RBMM
United States
214.987.6500
www.rbmm.com

Rick Johnson & Company
United States
505.266.1100
www.rjc.com

Rickabaugh Graphics
United States
614.337.2229
www.rickbaughgraphics.com

RIGGS
United States
803.799.5972
www.riggspeak.com

ROAD design inc.
United States
949.494.8020
www.roaddzn.com

ROBOT
United States
210.476.8801
www.robotcreative.com

Robot Agency Studios
United States
832.859.0650
www.robotagency.com

Roger Christian & Co.
United States
210.829.1953
www.warmsprings.org

Rome & Gold Creative
United States
505.897.0870
www.rgcreative.com

Ross Creative + Strategy
United States
309.637.7677
www.rosscps.com

Ross Hogin Design
United States
206.443.3930
www.hogin.com

Rotor Design
United States
763.706.3906
www.rotordesign.net

Rule29
United States
630.262.1009
www.rule29.com

Ryan Cooper
United States
303.917.9911

S Design, Inc.
United States
405.608.0556
www.sdesigninc.com

S4LE.com
Canada
905.467.7139
www.s4le.com

Sabet Branding
United States
949.705.9960
www.sabet.com

Sabingrafik, Inc.
United States
760.431.0439
www.tracy.sabin.com

Sakkal Design
United States
425.483.8830
www.sakkal.com

Sam's Garage
United States
720.320.7220
www.samsgarageonline.com

Sandstrom Design
United States
503.248.9466
www.sandstromdesign.com

sarah watson design
United States
206.545.8682
www.sarahwatsondesign.com

Savage Design Group
United States
713.522.1555
www.savagedesign.com

Savage Synapses Unltd.
United States
443.756.4674
www.flotsandjets.com

Sayles Graphic Design, Inc.
United States
515.279.2922
www.saylesdesign.com

Schuster Design Group
United States
214.632.3328

Scott Oeschger Design
United States
610.497.1101
www.scottoeschger.com

SD Graphic Design
United States
617.523.5144
www.delaneygroup.com

Seed Studios
United States
817.431.1405
www.seedstudios.com

Sergio Bianco
Italy
39.185.77.2289
www.sergiobianco.it

Sharp Communications, Inc.
United States
212.892.0002
www.sharpthink.com

sharp pixel
United States
206.226.1030
www.sharppixel.com

Shawn Hazen Graphic Design
United States
510.594.9271
www.shawnhazen.com

sheean design
United States
707.224.5206
www.sheeandesign.com

Shelley Design + Marketing
United States
410.523.2796
www.shelleyllc.com

Shift design
Portugal
351.21.410.5912
www.shiftdesign.pt

Sibley/ Peteet Design
United States
512.473.2333
www.spdaustin.com

silvercreativegroup
United States
203.855.7705
www.silvercreativegroup.com

Simon & Goetz Design
Germany
49.69.96.88.55.0
www.simongoetz.de

Sire Advertising
United States
570.743.3900
www.sireadvertising.com

SKOOTA
United States
919.824.6487
www.skoota.com

Sockeye Creative
United States
503.226.3843
www.sockeyecreative.com

Soho Joe
United States
612.588.8740
www.sohojoe.com

Solo Multimedia, Inc.
United States
785.841.5500
www.solomultimedia.com

Sommese Design
United States
814.353.1951

soupgraphix
United States
619.749.SOUP
www.soupgraphix.com

Special Modern Design
United States
323.258.1212
www.specialmoderndesign.com

Squires & Company
United States
214.939.9194
www.squirescompany.com

Stacy Bormett Design, LLC
United States
651.748.0872

Stand Advertising
United States
716.210.1065
www.standadvertising.com

Starlight Studio
United States
718.302.5600

Stephan and Herr
United States
717.426.2939
www.stephanherr.com

Sterling Brands
United States
212.329.4600
www.sterlingbrands.com

Steven O'Connor
United States
323.779.5600

Steve's Portfolio
United States
215.840.0880
www.stevesportfolio.net

Stiles + co
United States
503.806.4670
www.stilesandco.com

Stoltze Design
United States
617.350.7109
www.stoltze.com

Straka Dusan/Straka Design
Germany
49.179.126.8229
www.hofd.net

Strange Ideas
United States
316.259.4374

Strategic America
United States
515.453.2000
www.strategicamerica.com

Strategy Studio
United States
212.966.7800
www.strategy-studio.com

strategyone
United States
630.790.9050
www.strategyone.com

stressdesign
United States
315.422.3231
www.stressdesign.com

Studio Arts and Letters
United States
303.298.9911
www.studioartsandletters.com

Studio D
United States
212.563.5600
www.studiodny.com

Studio GT&P
Italy
39.074.232.0372
www.tobanelli.it

Studio Simon
United States
502.479.8447
www.studiosimon.net

Studio Stubborn Sideburn
United States
206.709.8970
www.stubbornsideburn.com

STUN Design and Advertising
United States
225.381.7266
www.stundesign.net

Stuph Clothing
United States
800.242.9166
www.uthstuph.com

Suburban Utopia
United States
706.425.8836
www.suburbanutopia.com

SUMO
United Kingdom
0191.261.9894
www.sumodesign.co.uk

Sutter Design
United States
301.459.5445
www.sutterdesign.com

switchfoot creative
United States
760.720.4255
www.switchfootcreative.com

Synergy Graphix
United States
212.968.7568
www.synergygraphix.com

Tactical Magic
United States
901.722.3001
www.tacticalmagic.com

Tactix Creative
United States
480.225.1480
www.tactixcreative.com

Tallgrass Studios
United States
785.887.6049
www.tallgrassstudios.com

tanagram partners
United States
312.876.3668
www.tanagram.com

TBF Creative
United States
602.722.7995
www.tbfcreative.com

Tchopshop Media
United States
504.895.0000
www.tchopshop.com

tesser inc.
United States
415.541.9999
www.tesser.com

the atmosfear
United States
702.355.8896
www.theatmosfear.com

The Clockwork Group
United States
210.798.1000
www.theclockworkgroup.com

The Collaboration
United States
913.271.3603
www.the-collaboration.com

The Design Poole
United States
206.301.9282
www.thedesignpoole.com

The Envision Group
United States
303.843.9777
www.envision-grp.com

The Flores Shop
United States
804.304.6731
www.thefloresshop.com

The Gate Worldwide
United States
212.508.3400
www.thegateworldwide.com

The Joe Bosack Graphic
Design Co.
United States
215.766.1461
www.joebosack.com

The Logo Factory Inc.
Canada
905.564.6747
www.thelogofactory.com

The Meyocks Group
United States
515.225.1200
www.outofthebox.com

The Oesterle
Germany
00.49.89.130.178.74
www.the-oesterle.com

The Pink Pear Design Company
United States
816.519.7327
www.pinkpear.com

The Robin Shepherd Group
United States
904.359.0981
www.trsg.net

The zen kitchen
United States
401.787.5178
www.daniordin.net

thehappycorp global
United States
646.613.1220
www.thehappycorp.com

Thielen Designs
United States
505.396.3900
www.ThielenDesigns.com

Think Tank Creative
United States
337.989.4018

Thomas Manss & Company
United Kingdom
44.20.7251.7777
www.manss.com

thomas-vasquez.com
United States
718.422.1948

Tiffany Design
United States
714.467.8428

Tim Frame Design
United States
937.766.3749
www.timframe.com

Times Infinity
United States
713.224.6200
www.times-infinity.com

Timpano Group
United States
608.251.0808
www.timpanogroup.com

Todd M. LeMieux
United States
413.747.9321
www.toddlemieux.com

Tom Fowler, Inc.
United States
203.845.0700
www.tomfowlerinc.com

Traci Jones design
United States
303.447.8202
www.commarts-boulder.com

Tribe Design
United States
713.523.5119
www.tribedesign.com

TungId Advertising Agency
Iceland
354.533.2323
www.tungl.is

Turner Duckworth
United States / United Kingdom
415.675.7777
44.0.20.8994.7190
www.TurnerDuckworth.com

Turney Creative
United States
858.349.6370
www.turneycreative.com

Type G
United States
858.792.7333
www.typegdesign.com

Typonic
United Kingdom
44.13.7655.4823
www.typonic.com

Uhlein Design
United States
215.206.2733
www.uhleindesign.com

UlrichPinciotti Design Group
United States
419.255.4515
www.updesigngroup.com

UltraVirgo Creative
United States
646.638.0813
www.ultravirgo.com

Unibrand Belgrade
Turkmenistan
993.81.11.3285.257
www.unibrand360.com

Univisual
Italy
39.02.668.4268
www.univisual.it

UNO
United States
612.874.1920
www.unoonline.com

urbanINFLUENCE
design studio
United States
206.219.3599
www.urbaninfluence.com

V V N Design
United States
706.903.2410
www.vvndesign.com

Velocity Design Works
Canada
204.475.0514
www.velocitydesignworks.com

Vigor Graphic Design, LLC.
United States
717.234.4846
www.vigorgraphics.net

Vincent Burkhead Studio
United States
619.787.9384
www.VincentBurkhead.com

Visual Coolness
United States
520.722.6364
www.visualcoolness.com

Visual Inventor Ltd. Co.
United States
405.842.6768
www.VisualInventor.com

Visual Moxie
United States
805.277.4741
www.visualmoxie.com

VMA
United States
937.233.7500
www.vmai.com

Wallace Church, Inc.
United States
212.755.2903
www.wallacechurch.com

Walsh Associates
United States
918.743.9600
www.walshassoc.com

Wells Fargo Financial
United States
515.557.7825

Werner Design Werks
United States
612.338.2550
www.wdw.com

Weylon Smith
United States
615.306.1485

Whaley Design, Ltd
United States
651.645.3463
www.whaleydesign.com

Whence: the studio
United States
504.338.2994
www.michaelnixdesign.com

Whitney Edwards LLC
United States
410.822.8335
www.wedesign.com

Wholesale Distributors
United States
206.290.7017
www.wd-usa.com

Who's the Min/
Creative Solutions
United States
973.219.2335
www.whosthemin.com

Wilkinson Media, Inc.
United States
609.818.0363
www.wilkinsonmedia.net

Willoughby Design Group
United States
816.561.4189
www.willoughbydesign.com

Wolken communica
United States
206.545.1696
www.wolkencommunica.com

Wolff Olins
United Kingdom
44.0.20.7713.7733
www.wolff-olins.com

Wray Ward Laseter
United States
704.332.9071
www.wwlcreative.com

www.iseedots.com
United States
619.955.8178
www.iseedots.com

Yellobee Studio
United States
404.249.6407
www.yellobee.com

Yellow Fin Studio
United States
512.472.3227
www.yellowfinstudio.com

Yellow Pencil
Brand Sharpening
New Zealand
64.365.0080
www.yellowpencil.co.nz

ykcreative, LLC
United States
832.752.6402
www.ykcreative.com

Zapata Design
United States
281.785.0242
www.zapatadesign.com

ZEBRA Design Branding
Russia
7.8482.485684

Zed + Zed + Eye
Creative Communications
United States
352.572.3474
www.zedzedeye.com

zengigi design
United States
301.562.9406
www.zengigi.com

Zipper Design
United States
206.818.9101
www.zipperd.com

Zombie Design
United States
801.299.1567
www.designzombie.com

ZONA Design
United States
212.244.2900
www.zonadesign.com

Zwölf Sonnen Design
Germany
49.06.114.504.942
www.zwoelfsonnen.de

about the authors

Bill Gardner is president of Gardner Design and has produced work for Learjet, Thermos, Nissan, Pepsi, Pizza Hut, Kroger, Hallmark, Cargill Corporation, and the 2004 Athens Olympics. His work has been featured in *Communication Arts*, *Print*, *Graphis*, *New York Art Directors Annual*, *Step Inside Design*, Mead Top 60, the Museum of Modern Art, and many other national and international design exhibitions. He lives in Wichita, Kansas.

Cathy Fishel is a freelance writer and editor who specializes in graphic design. She is the author of many books on the subject; contributes to many magazines, including *PRINT* and *Communication Arts*; and is editor of LogoLounge.com.

John Harrold

CONTENTS

RUPERT, BEPPO & THE KITE BY ALFRED BESTALL
ALL OTHER STORIES BY JAMES HENDERSON
ILLUSTRATED BY JOHN HARROLD
STORY COLOURING BY DORIS CAMPBELL

John Harrold

**This Book
Belongs To:**

ISBN 0-85079-179-0

RUPERT

THE DAILY EXPRESS ANNUAL

John Harrold.

Published by Express Newspapers p.l.c., Fleet Street, EC4P 4JT

RUPERT

Says Tigerlily one fine day,
"A friend of yours has come to stay."

School is over for the week and Nutwood's youngsters pour through the gates, chattering happily about their plans for the weekend. "I must hurry home," Tigerlily, the Chinese Conjurer's daughter, tells Rupert. "We have a very honoured visitor. It is someone you know – the Sage of Um." "The Sage of Um!" echoes Rupert. "Oh, I must come and say 'Hello' to him." And so the chums set out for Tigerlily's pagoda home.

on Um Island

"From his far island home he's come.
You know him well – the Sage of Um!"

Rupert decides that he must go
To see the Sage and say, "Hello".

As they go, Rupert recalls the times he has met the funny old Sage and his flying craft, the Brella. "But, in fact," he winds up, "I know almost nothing about him, not even what Um is." "Oh, I know it is an island and that the Sage is the only *person* who lives there," Tigerlily says. Rupert wants to ask what she means by "only *person*", but by then they have reached her home and he is being ushered in to greet the Sage.

So Tigerlily takes her chum
To see his friend, the Sage of Um.

RUPERT IS OFFERED A TRIP

The Sage – when Ruperts asks him where
His home is – says he'll take him there.

There's no need for delay and so
To ask his parents off they go.

When Rupert asks them if he may
Go with the Sage, "Of course!" they say.

So first thing next day, sharp and bright,
Rupert is ready for the flight.

The Sage is delighted to see Rupert. 'Why, the little bear who has adventures!' he cries. "Each time we have met there has been adventure afoot." "Not this time!" laughs Rupert. Then Tigerlily chips in: "Honourable Sage, Rupert is very curious about your island of Um . . ." At that, the Sage jumps up with a cry of "Then you shall visit it, Rupert! We can go tomorrow and be back for Sunday tea. Let's ask your parents!" And, mind awhirl, Rupert finds himself being hustled to his cottage by the Sage.

Mr. and Mrs. Bear have never met the Sage and at first don't know what to make of this jolly old man who wants to take Rupert to visit his home. But they have heard Rupert talk of him, he is so charming and Um sounds so nice that they say, yes. And next morning, with his overnight things in a case, Rupert is hurrying up to the Conjurer's pagoda where the Sage is waiting with Tigerlily and the Brella.

RUPERT SEES A UNICORN

Then in the Sage's Brella they
Are soon airborne and on their way.

"There's Um, and very soon you'll see
Who share my island home with me."

"Down there!" cries Rupert. "Now I know!
A pony – wait! But is it, though?"

Now Rupert can't believe his eyes.
"No! It's a unicorn!" he cries.

Rupert has travelled before in the Sage's craft, the Brella, and knows what to expect. He has no sooner settled beside the Sage than the Bella is curving into the air, leaving Nutwood a huddle of houses far below. Soon the coast is left behind and they are racing over the ocean. After a while Rupert asks the question he has been longing to put: "Tigerlily says you are the only *person* on Um. What else lives on it?" But just then Um comes into sight.

"Oh, it *is* lovely!" Rupert breathes as the Brella slows and he can really see the island. The Sage smiles and says, "You were asking what, other than myself, lives here. Let's take a look, shall we?" Down goes the Brella in a low swoop. At first there is no sign of movement, then a flash of something catches Rupert's eye. "A pony! You have ponies!" he cries. "No!" laughs the Sage and brings the Brella nearer the galloping creature. Rupert gasps: "It's a unicorn!"

RUPERT IS ALARMED

"But there's a herd. Where can they be?"
The Sage cries. "Let's go down and see!

But no! They soar back in the air.
There's something very wrong down there!

Then as they hover near his cave,
"That's smoke!" the Sage cries, very grave.

Now closer to the smoke they go
And spy the lost herd down below.

"Yes, a unicorn!" chuckles the Sage. "Now you know what I share Um Island with – a small herd of unicorns, the only ones in the world!" "But where are the others?" Rupert asks. "Indeed, where *are* they?" echoes the Sage. "The one we saw is the leader and the others usually stay close to it. Let's land near my cave and have a look." So down goes the Brella and it is just about to land when the Sage swerves it back into a climb. "Something's wrong down there!" he says.

The Brella circles back towards the Sage's cave but stops and hovers some way from it. The Sage points to puffs of smoke rising from a nearby clump of trees. "Unicorns can't light fires," he says quietly. "And no one else should be here." Very slowly the Sage edges the Brella closer to the trees. Rupert gasps at what he sees. The trees form a short tunnel leading to a sort of paddock enclosed by rocks. In it, huddled together, are the missing unicorns!

8

RUPERT IS GRABBED

So down our two come and set out
To find what this is all about.

So that's what caused the smoke and made
The cowering unicorns afraid!

The Sage says that he knows who's there –
Just then two large hands grab our pair.

"My master, the Enchanter, wants
To meet you two," the huge man taunts.

The Sage puts a finger to his lip and points downwards. Rupert nods. They are going to land and must be silent. Gently as a feather, the Sage lands the Brella some way from the trees. The two climb out and head for the puffs of smoke past shrubs and flowers such as Rupert has never seen. When they reach the clump of trees and see what is scaring the unicorns Rupert's eyes pop. It is a fire-breathing dragon. And on its back it has two saddles.

"Aha!" breathes the Sage. "Now I know who is here! The one who rides a dragon and has long envied me my unicorns . . ." But at that moment Rupert yelps with fright. He has been grabbed by his jersey. In the same moment a large hand seizes the Sage's collar and a voice booms, "Correct! It is my master, the great Enchanter!" The speaker is a huge man whose head is shaved but for a thin plume of hair held by a ring. He propels our two towards the Sage's cave.

9

Inside the Sage's cave our pair
Are dragged up to a throne-like chair.

Rupert's astounded at the sight
Of who climbs down into the light.

When Rupert gasps, "Why, it's a boy!"
The other yells – but not with joy!

And when the Sage tries to explain,
He starts to rant and rave again.

The huge man bundles Rupert and the Sage into the cave where a lamp casts a pool of light. Around it are deep shadows. Among them Rupert can see a tall chair like a throne. The friends are dumped in the pool of light and the big man addresses the chair, "O, great Enchanter, behold the prisoners you have been expecting." Something rises from the chair. Rupert holds his breath. Then he gasps at the sight of the figure who steps into the light.

"It's a boy!" blurts out Rupert. And, indeed, the "great" Enchanter, smirking triumphantly, does not look much older than Rupert. But at Rupert's words his smirk vanishes and he screams, "Never, never say that again!" "Say what?" quavers Rupert. "That he is what you said he was," explains the Sage quietly. "He's as old as me. But when he was an apprentice enchanter . . ." "ENOUGH!" the Enchanter squeals. "You shall mock me no more, Sage, when you learn what I mean to do!"

RUPERT IS LOCKED UP

"For strongest spells I need the horns
Of your – the only – unicorns!"

"I've got them all, except for one.
I'll get that too, and then you're done!"

"Why does he," Rupert asks the Sage,
"Still look a boy, although your age."

"When learning about time with me,
He got things wrong, as you can see."

With a nasty grin, the tiny Enchanter reveals his plans: "The most powerful magic in the world can only be made with unicorn horn. I need that magic, but you, Sage, have refused to let me have any . . ." "Without horns the unicorns would die!" protests the Sage. The Enchanter sneers: "Well, I need beg no more! When I have caught the one still at large I shall have all the unicorns in the world. Then I shall deal with you. Meantime you'll be locked up."

The Sage and Rupert are bundled into an inner cave where the Sage finishes explaining why the Enchanter never grew up: "He's always been too smart for his own good even when he was learning magic. One day, despite being warned not to, he tried out a spell for moving you back and forward in time. He got it wrong and has stayed as he is ever since. The trouble is that he has believed for ages that a potion using unicorn horn will undo the spell he is under."

RUPERT IS GIVEN A TASK

"That hole leads to the outer air.
Someone like you can climb out there."

"We have to thwart him and so you
Must do what I shall tell you to."

"Wear that. Put this ring on its horn.
You'll speak to any unicorn."

"Find their leader that's free and say
It must lure the dragon guard away."

"But enough talk," cries the Sage. "We must save the unicorns. Here's what you must do . . ." "Me?" squeaks Rupert. For answer the Sage points to a hole in the cave roof. "That lets air into this, my larder. A good small climber could get out that way and find the unicorn leader. Together they might lure away the dragon and free the others. In order to talk to the unicorn . . ." He produces from his pouch a large ring on a chain and a thing like a headband. He places the headband on Rupert's forehead and says, "With this on you can 'talk' to the unicorn just by thinking what you want to say. To hear its replies put this ring on its horn and hold the chain." "Maybe I can get the unicorns to attack the dragon," suggests Rupert. "Dear me, no!" the Sage says. "Unicorns are far too timid. You'll have enough to do getting their leader to help you. Now, off you go!" And Rupert starts his climb to the outside.

12

RUPERT CONTACTS THE LEADER

Now up the steep shaft Rupert goes,
Balancing on hands and toes.

"I hope the one that's free is not
As scared stiff as that timid lot."

Now Rupert makes his way to where
He saw the leader from the air.

As told to, he "thinks" his command.
At once the unicorn's at hand.

The rocky shaft out of the cave is steep and just wide enough to let Rupert scramble up it. Above him he can see bright daylight and before long he climbs out into the open to find that he is looking down on the captive unicorns. Puffs of smoke from the guardian dragon still rise from the trees in front of them. Rupert can see how right the Sage was about unicorns being timid. They look terrified. "Let's hope their leader's a bit braver," he thinks.

The Sage has suggested that Rupert look for the unicorn leader where they first saw it, and that's where Rupert heads. He thinks, "I'll get the leader to let the dragon see it. If it taunts the beast enough the dragon won't be able to resist chasing it. Then I'll get the others to run for it." When he feels that he has reached the right place Rupert stops and thinks a message to the unicorn's leader: "The Sage has sent me. Come!" There is a whinny behind him.

RUPERT RIDES THE UNICORN

To understand the unicorn
He slips the ring onto its horn.

"Me, lure the dragon? That's your plan?"
It whinnies. "I'm not sure I can."

So Rupert "thinks" his sternest voice
And tells it that it has no choice.

But he himself feels far from brave
As they head for the Sage's cave.

Rupert and the unicorn stare at each other. Then Rupert slips the ring the Sage gave him over the creature's horn. At once he hears a whimper: "Oh, dear, I'm far too frightened to do it." "Do what?" cries Rupert. "Why, get the dragon to chase me," comes the answer. The unicorn sees Rupert's look of astonishment and goes on, "Remember, while you are wearing the headband I know what you are thinking. And that *is* what you've been planning to do, isn't it?"

Just as Rupert feared, the unicorn leader is both timid and tiresome. "Why weren't *you* caught?" he demands. "I'm swifter than the rest and I know every inch of Um," it replies. "Then if you can do it once you can do it again," Rupert tells it firmly. "After all, you're the leader. Now, let's go. And to save time I'll ride on your back." He takes the ring and scrambles onto the back of the unicorn. He grasps the creature's mane and off they gallop to the Sage's cave.

RUPERT STARTS HIS PLAN

The unicorn slows when it sees
The dragon's smoke above the trees.

"Stay there until you hear me say,
'Come on!' There must be no delay."

The herd's still captive, still forlorn.
Rupert calls up the unicorn.

With taunting whinny it appears.
The dragon can't believe its ears.

Even before the Sage's cave comes into view the timid unicorn is galloping more slowly. When it sees the dragon's smoke above the trees it slows to a trot. And it is very ready to stop at Rupert's command. Using the headband Rupert tells it, "Stay here while I take a look. Listen for my command. When you hear it, don't delay. Come to where the dragon can see you and taunt it into chasing you." As he sets off he turns to see the unicorn looking fearfully after him.

Feeling far from brave himself and wishing he were back in Nutwood Rupert steals up on the dragon. Gosh, it *is* fearsome! With each puff of smoke from its snout the unicorns whinny in fear. "Well, no use wasting time," decides Rupert. He concentrates. "Rupert to unicorn leader," he thinks. "Now!" For a long moment nothing happens. Then, with a taunting whinny, the unicorn leader capers into view. Startled, the dragon swings round towards it.

RUPERT FREES THE UNICORNS

It means to make this unicorn
Wish that it never had been born.

But now, although the way is clear,
The unicorns still cower in fear.

So Rupert "calls" through his headband,
"Run, unicorns! That's my command!"

Too late the trick the dragon sees
As all the unicorn herd flees.

The dragon can't believe this. A unicorn, one of those wretched creatures, challenging the great Enchanter's dragon! It is so astounded it doesn't move and Rupert wonders if it might refuse to be lured. But just then the unicorn leader gives a particularly offensive whinny. That does it! With one last puff of smoke at the captives, the dragon bounds after its tormentor. "Run!" Rupert shouts at the unicorns. But they stay put, huddled and scared. Then he sees that perhaps his shouting is confusing the creatures. He presses the headband to his brow and thinks hard: "Unicorns, I am Rupert, a friend of the Sage. I command you to flee while the dragon is away!" Next moment they are racing past him and past the dragon which has just seen, too late, that it has been tricked. There are so many of them it doesn't know where to turn. The Enchanter and his slave, hearing all the noise, race out of the cave.

16

RUPERT LETS THE SAGE OUT

Now the Enchanter and his slave
Rush furiously from the cave.

Luckily they have left the key,
And Rupert sets his old friend free.

Outside they see the wicked pair
Order their mount into the air.

To save the herd they must give chase,
So to the Brella our two race.

The Enchanter is squealing with rage as he sees the unicorns disappearing, and Rupert waits until he is well out of the way before he leaves his hiding place and scurries to the cave. One last look after the Enchanter to make sure he has not been seen, then he darts into the cave and makes for the inner chamber. Luckily the key has been left in the door. In a moment the Sage is free and exclaiming, "Well done! Now we must get after that wicked pair!"

Rupert and the Sage emerge from the cave to see that the Enchanter and his slave have mounted the dragon. Rupert almost feels sorry for it, the Enchanter is raging at it so for being tricked. "Oh, you shall pay for this!" he shrieks. "Now, get after them!" He digs his heels hard into the dragon's sides, the beast flaps its wings and takes off. "Quick! to the Brella!" cries the Sage. "At all costs we must stop the Enchanter attacking the unicorns!"

RUPERT STOPS THE DRAGON

The Brella sweeps into the air.
And there's the dragon over there!

The unicorns are in a pack
And far too easy to attack.

The dragon dives. Our pair pursue.
There's only one thing they can do.

They dive straight for its fiery snout
And force the beast to swing about.

Rupert and the Sage race to where they left the Brella and scramble aboard. The Sage twiddles part of the Brella's handle and before Rupert can blink the craft is high above the trees. Higher still is the Enchanter's dragon. It moves fast and the Brella is hard pressed to catch up. Before it can, the dragon dives and Rupert sees why. It is heading for the fleeing unicorns. The stupid things have stayed together making themselves an easy target. If only they had scattered the Enchanter wouldn't have known which way to go. Now he has them. "Attack!" he screams. "Stop them anyhow!" Breathing flames, the dragon swoops on the terrified unicorns. "Hold tight!" the Sage cries and the Brella dives, faster and steeper than the dragon. Just when it seems the dragon's flames will scorch the unicorns, the Brella swoops under its snout and the great beast, with a startled roar and flapping of wings, has to swerve aside.

RUPERT BALES OUT

The dragon swerves but turns right back
And races in to the attack.

It gives the Brella such a clout
That Rupert and the Sage fall out.

The Sage hangs on and down they float
With Rupert clinging to his coat.

The dragon with its nasty crew
Comes down a few feet from our two.

The unicorns have been saved from the dragon's attack, and Rupert can see them scatter among the trees. For a moment, too, it looks as if the Enchanter is giving up the chase, for his dragon seems to be heading away from the scene. In fact, he's far from done. The dragon is only giving itself room to attack. It makes a great sweeping turn then heads for the Brella. Before the Sage can get it out of the way the Brella is swiped by a great wing and capsized.

Then everything happens at once. The Brella turns upside-down. The Sage grabs the handle. Rupert catches the Sage's hem with one hand and with the other his case which has been in the Brella all the time. Down they float with the Brella as a parachute and Rupert trying very hard not to show how frightened he is and how much he wishes he were safe at home. But they reach the ground unharmed. Unfortunately, at the same moment so does the dragon!

Says the Enchanter with a grin,
"This time, O, Sage, I think I win!"

But what is this? The unicorns
Advance with deadly levelled horns.

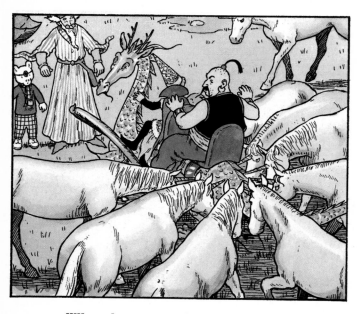

When they can prod the dragon's sides,
Onto the scene their leader strides.

"Destroy the wretched unicorn!"
The dragon's told. But there's that horn!

The Enchanter smirks. "You have often crossed my path, Sage," he pipes. "And until now you have always won. Now I am going to get rid of you and this bear then I shall recapture those wretched unicorns and the magic of their horns shall be mine." Rupert daren't think what is in store for him and the Sage. But there is a nasty glint in the dragon's eyes. "I'm not going to let them see how scared I am," he thinks. Just then from the trees emerge the unicorns!

Everyone is too astounded to speak. The only sound is the pad of hooves. The unicorns are nothing like the frightened things Rupert last saw. Horns levelled like spears, they close on the dragon. Last comes their leader looking, if anything, more threatening. It halts only when its horn is an inch from the dragon's face. The Enchanter is the first to find his voice. "Don't stand there!" he screeches at the dragon. "I order you – destroy the unicorn!"

RUPERT'S FRIEND TRIUMPHS

"Yes, burn it!" the Enchanter cries.
Poor Rupert has to shut his eyes.

He hears a sob and risks a peek.
A tear rolls down the dragon's cheek.

He's beaten, the Enchanter knows.
And with that all his spirit goes.

And now he learns he mustn't scorn
Even the gentle unicorn.

Rupert can't remember having seen anyone quite as angry as the Enchanter. His face is twisted with rage as he squeals at the dragon. "Fire, I say! Destroy it!" Smoke trickles from the dragon's nostrils. The gentle unicorn and the beastly dragon glare into each other's faces. Rupert has to cover his eyes. He waits for the fiery roar. But nothing. He risks opening an eye. And he can scarcely believe it. A large tear is running down the dragon's snout.

That tear is just the first of many, and as the dragon sobs, smiles spread on the faces of Rupert and the Sage. Suddenly all the fizz goes out of the Enchanter and he seems like nothing more dangerous than a particularly nasty small boy. Now the Sage takes over. "You unpleasant little thing," he storms, "this is our last battle and you have lost, thanks to the gentle unicorns you despised." The Enchanter slumps in his saddle. There is nothing he can say.

RUPERT ASKS A QUESTION

"They won't forget this lesson so,"
The Sage declares, "they're free to go."

"That 'great' Enchanter won't again
Stray very far from his domain."

"Now," Rupert says, "I must be told,
What made you unicorns so bold?"

"Although I acted brave, they knew –
By this – that I was frightened too."

"Let them go," the Sage tells Rupert. "This so-called 'great' Enchanter and his dragon have been beaten by the gentlest of creatures, unicorns. From now on among magicians and sages his name will be a joke. I don't think he will stray far from his domain." So, using his headband, Rupert orders the unicorns to fall back. "Begone!" the Sage commands the Enchanter who gulps an order to his sobbing dragon. It lumbers into the air and has soon dwindled into the distance.

The very next thing Rupert does is slip the ring over the unicorn leader's horn and ask, "Well, how did you all suddenly turn bold?" His smile grows as he listens to the reply. Then he turns to the Sage and says. "When I wore the headband they heard *all* my thoughts, not just those I meant for them. They knew I was as scared as they were but kept going and tried not to show it. So they felt ashamed and decided that if I could do it, so could they. And it worked!"

RUPERT FLIES HOME

Now the Enchanter's gone they feel
It's time that they enjoyed a meal.

The Sage says the Enchanter may
Learn how he can grow up one day.

The unicorns all turn out when
Rupert sets off for home again.

Mr. and Mrs. Bear are there
To welcome the returning pair.

With the Enchanter banished and the unicorns free to roam Um Island again, Rupert realises how hungry he is. The Sage is peckish too, and so the pair fly back to the cave for a meal. As they eat, Rupert asks, "Will the Enchanter ever grow up?" The Sage replies, "He could. And it wouldn't need magic. All that's needed is for him to stop thinking and acting like a particularly unpleasant small boy." "And will he?" Rupert asks. "I hope so," says the Sage.

Next day Rupert and the Sage leave for Nutwood. As the Brella heads out to sea, the unicorns gather to see them off. "You taught them something important," the Sage tells Rupert. "You showed them that being brave isn't the same thing as not being afraid." Rupert is still pondering that remark as the Brella sweeps in to land near his cottage. "Brave? Me?" he thinks. "Really?" But what he says is, "Oh, look! There's Mummy and Daddy waiting for us!" The End.

RUPERT

Rupert and Algy call one day
On Bingo to come out to play.

Rupert and Algy call on their chum Bingo one morning, hoping he'll come out to play. They find him busy in his workshop. "Coming out to play, Bingo?" Rupert calls. "No thanks. Too busy," the clever pup shouts back. "Got to test this. Come and have a look." "A go-cart!" exclaim the others when they join Bingo. "And it's a beauty," Rupert says. Bingo grins: "Well, I must say I *am* rather proud of it."

and the Go-Cart

"No thanks," says Bingo. "I must start
To try out this, my new go-cart."

"A go-cart does sound lots of fun,"
Says Algy. "Why don't we build one?"

A little later Rupert and Algy are walking away from Bingo's house when Algy says, "A go-cart does sound lots of fun. Why don't we have a go at making one?" "But where do we get wood, wheels and stuff?" Rupert asks. And they are still puzzling over this when they spot the little servant of their clever friend, the Professor. "Come on!" Algy cries. "Let's ask if the Professor's got anything we could use!"

The old Professor's servant! He
May know where useful bits may be.

RUPERT IS OFFERED HELP

"Why, yes!" he gives a happy shout.
"We've lots that's due to be thrown out."

"This old shed is just full of stuff.
I feel quite sure you'll find enough."

"When his inventions fail, I fear,
He simply dumps the bits in here."

"Don't know what they're supposed to do,
But surely they'd make wheels for you."

"What a coincidence!" cries the little servant when Rupert and Algy catch up with him and ask. "The fact is, my master, the Professor, has told me to clear out a lot of stuff that's been left over from his experiments. I'm sure that among it there are bound to be wheels and wood and the like." The pals grin at each other. They can't believe their luck as the servant leads the way to a shed behind the Professor's tower home. "This place is full of stuff," he says.

And isn't he right! The pals gasp when they see inside the shed. The servant chuckles: "You know what my master's like! One experiment or invention after another. Some work, some don't. But sooner or later the parts end up here." He pauses and looks around. "Now, wheels . . ." he muses. "Ah, yes!" He rummages in a pile and comes up with two bits of machinery. "I don't know what these were meant to do," he says. "But surely they'll make wheels for you."

RUPERT SEES THE STRANGE BOX

There's lots of wood and bolts and screws,
So many things the pals can use.

"This box won't open. Still, it's neat,
And it would make a splendid seat."

A barrow's brought then so that they
Can take their go-cart stuff away.

"I think the wheels, though seeming good,
Just didn't work quite as they should."

The wheels the servant has dug out are oddly thick and have curious axles. But they look just the thing for a go-cart, Rupert and Algy agree. So now they set about looking for wood, bolts, nuts and screws to make the body. Rupert is busy dragging out several stout planks when Algy says, "Look at this box I've found. I can't open it but it's just the thing for a seat. And if the lid's nailed down as tight as all that it should be all the stronger, shouldn't it?"

At last Rupert and Algy have all they need to build a go-cart and the little servant says, "Now let's find something to carry it in." And off he goes to return with a wheelbarrow which the pals load with their stuff. "What did the Professor use all this for?" Rupert asks. "The nuts and bolts are just nuts and bolts," the servant says. "The box, I think, came from an explorer friend. The wheels . . . the Professor said something about them not working as he'd hoped."

RUPERT IS LENT A WORKSHOP

"Round here's a workshop you may use
To build your go-cart if you choose."

"The old Professor's very kind.
You may be sure that he won't mind."

"Do use the tools but put them back,
When you are finished, in the rack."

"This stuff is great," says Rupert, "but
Why is this box so tightly shut?"

Even if the wheel things didn't live up to the Professor's hopes, the pals are sure they will be just the thing for them. Now the question is, where are they going to build their go-cart? "I can help with that, too!" the servant says. "At the other end of this building is a workshop that isn't used now. I know the Professor won't mind you using it." And off he scampers ahead of the pals and their wheelbarrow to throw open the workshop doors. "There!" he announces.

The old workshop is all the two young go-cart builders could wish. "You may work here until teatime then come back tomorrow," the servant tells them. "Put the tools back neatly and lock up when you go." Then off he trots. Algy picks up one of the pairs of wheels and studies them. He spins one. "They move beautifully," he says. "And they're much lighter than they look." Rupert examines the box Algy found. "Odd that it should be nailed up so tight," he muses.

RUPERT GETS DOWN TO WORK

At once, with spanner, saw and drill,
The two pals set to with a will.

When they lock up that night they say,
They'll finish their go-cart next day.

His Mummy tells the little bear,
"It all sounds fun but do take care."

Rupert's still puzzled late that night:
"Why has that box been shut so tight?"

Now Rupert and Algy get down to work on the go-cart. They decide on a plan and measure up the wood. Then Rupert saws it into lengths and Algy drills holes to take bolts for the axles of the strange wheels. They work on steadily until their tummies tell them it's teatime. By then, all that's left to do is to put the bits together and that, they decide, can wait until tomorrow. As he locks up the shed Rupert says, "I think it's going to be better than Bingo's."

"It sounds fun," says Mrs. Bear when Rupert tells his parents about the go-cart. "But are you sure the Professor won't mind you using his things?" She is quite happy, though, when Rupert assures her the things were going to be thrown out, anyway, and just says, "Well, do take care."

Later in bed Rupert gets to wondering again about the box they're using as a seat. "If it's going to be thrown out why is it shut so tight?" he thinks. "Very odd, I must say."

RUPERT'S PAL TESTS THE CART

By next day, when they break to eat,
The pals' go-cart is near complete.

"My master's sure to be amused
To see how his old junk's been used."

But our two pals can't wait to start
And test their splendid new go-cart.

The cart goes well, that much is proved,
But in the seat-box something moved!

First thing next day Rupert and Algy are back in the shed to start assembling the go-cart. They've brought sandwiches so that they need not go home for lunch. In fact, by the time they come to eat them the go-cart is almost ready. When they have eaten, they fix a pair of old handles to the seat and add a steering line to the front axle. As they wheel out the finished cart the servant appears. "Oh, my master will want to see that! I'll go and fetch him," he says.

But Algy and Rupert can't wait before trying out the go-cart. "Just a short run," Algy says. "Yes, to be sure it works," Rupert grins. "You go first." So, at the top of a gentle slope, Algy seats himself on the box and takes the steering line. "Right!" Rupert cries. He pushes and away goes the go-cart, gathering speed. But when it stops at the foot of the slope Algy gets off looking thoughtful. "Something's moving in that box," he tells Ruperts as he runs up.

30

RUPERT TRIES IT OUT

Says Algy, "Something bumped around!"
But Rupert can't hear any sound.

"Right," Algy says, "let's see if you,
When going fast, can hear it too."

This time they use a steeper slope
To reach a greater speed, they hope.

"Hey, stop!" rings out an anxious shout.
Too late. The go-cart's now flat-out!

"Not only did something bump in the box," Algy says. "When I got up speed the wheels made a whirring sound." Rupert puts his ear to the box but he can hear nothing. "Maybe it happens only when the go-cart's moving fast," Algy suggests. "Have a go and see if you notice anything." So they take the go-cart to a steeper slope where it should go even faster. As he gets ready Rupert remembers his earlier puzzlement about the box being shut so tight. But just then Algy cries,

"Ready!", gives a push and away races the go-cart. For a moment the speed is almost frightening, then just as Rupert starts to enjoy it, three things happen. From inside the box comes a very definite bump. The wheels start to whirr louder and louder. And from somewhere behind him Rupert hears the frantic voices of the Professor and his servant shouting for him to stop. That's much easier said than done, for now the go-cart is going flat-out!

RUPERT TAKES OFF

*Each of the go-cart's four wheels whirrs
And in the seat-box something stirs!*

*A cliff-top looms! No time to steer!
He's on the edge – and racing clear!*

*Now Rupert sees the reason why
There was no crash – the cart can fly!*

*The clever old Professor's made
Each wheel a sort of rotor-blade!*

Now everything's happening far too fast – the wheels whirring louder than ever, the Professor shouting, the bumping inside the box and the awful thought that in their hurry, Algy and he have fitted no brakes to the go-cart! Suddenly the whirring stops and, open-mouthed, Rupert sees the wheels begin to open like umbrellas! At the same moment he sees he is headed for a small cliff. No time to steer away from it! Next instant the go-cart sails over the edge of the cliff.

Rupert braces himself for a crash. But there is none – for the go-cart is flying! The wheels have opened completely and turned on their sides, whirring away like the rotor-blades of a helicopter. Rupert clings to the handles and holds his breath. But nothing awful happens. The wheels spin on, carrying the go-cart smoothly through the air just clear of the treetops. "I say," thinks Rupert. "I'm beginning to enjoy this, after all."

RUPERT THINKS HE SHOULD LAND

Now Rupert laughs, "I think I'll start
To call this thing my helicart!"

But Rupert's fun does not last long.
Once more that bumping! This time strong.

Below he sees his little band
Of friends and thinks, "I'd better land."

"Land? Oh, dear, I don't know how!
And, gosh, the bumping's much worse now!"

In no time at all Rupert begins to feel quite chirpy. He even makes a little joke – "I think I'll call this my helicart." He feels confident enough to let go of the handles and take up the steering line. He tries steering and it works. "I'll steer as far as Tigerlily's house," he decides. "Then I'll turn round." But it is just as he is rounding the pagoda that the bumping starts inside the box again. This time, though, it is much stronger! Rupert is not too worried about this because the go-cart is still flying well. He turns back to where he started and there, above the little cliff, he sees his three friends gazing up at him. The Professor seems to be shouting and Rupert remembers how, just before the go-cart took off, the Professor was trying to stop him. "I'd better land," he thinks. And with a shock he realises he doesn't know *how* to land! At that moment the bumping in the box becomes frighteningly stronger.

RUPERT GETS A SHOCK

It's just as well he cannot hear
The old Professor's cries of fear.

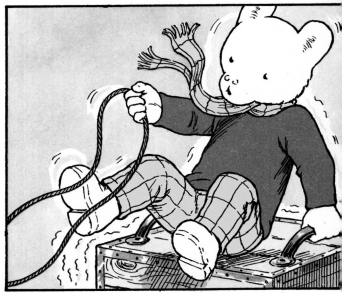

By now the bumping is so bad
That just to keep his seat he's glad.

Then suddenly all four wheels stop!
The helicart begins to drop!

Still louder comes the bumping sound
As Rupert plummets to the ground.

It's just as well that Rupert can't hear what the Professor is shouting which is, "Come down at once – you are in great danger!" Already he is quite scared enough and, anyway, he doesn't know *how* to bring the go-cart down. From inside the box comes a growing bump – bump – bump, and it shakes so much that Rupert has to grab a handle to stay put. "How *am* I going to land?" he quavers. Then he gives a cry of alarm, for he has just seen how he is likely to get down! The wheels which have been keeping the go-cart in the air have stopped! The go-cart slows. The rush of air dies away. The only sound comes from the box. Bump – bump – bump! Louder and stronger than ever. Then down drops the go-cart, so suddenly that it almost leaves poor Rupert behind. But he is clinging to the handles just as hard as he can and goes with it. Down – down – down the go-cart plummets. As the ground rushes up to meet it Rupert shuts his eyes.

RUPERT IS SAVED

Aghast, his poor friends watch the fall.
There's nothing they can do at all.

But now what's happening to the cart?
The seat-box seems to fly apart!

Two strange wings pop out from inside.
The cart's fall stops and down they glide.

As Rupert's craft comes in to land
His friends rush up to lend a hand.

On the ground Rupert's horrified friends watch the go-cart falling. There is not a thing they can do. Eyes shut tight, Rupert clings to the handles. He can't think. Just wait for the awful . . . Hello! What's happening? The bumping inside the box is frantic now. It's as if the box is going to tear itself apart. Cre-e-eak! Crack! Rupert risks opening an eye. Bits of wood fly past his face. But wait! The go-cart is not falling. It seems to be flying again! Rupert opens both eyes. Then he opens them really wide, astounded by what he sees. The go-cart *is* flying. But the wheels are still not working. And from holes in the side of the box protrude two wings. Such wings! They are like no bird's wings Rupert has ever seen. They look webbed and leathery, more like a bat's than a bird's. But they are plainly strong wings, for beating with a slow steady stroke, they carry the go-cart in a glide towards the ground.

Whatever's in the box can't see,
And so lands rather clumsily.

His friends help up the little bear,
But half-way, stop and gasp and stare!

And Rupert can't believe his eyes.
"Is that some sort of bird?" he cries.

The old man breathes, "I do declare,
That is a pterodactyl there!"

Whatever is in the box plainly can't see where it is flying, Rupert realises, and so, as the ground approaches he gets ready for the big bump. In fact, it isn't awful, but still enough to throw him clear of the go-cart. "Rupert, are you all right?" It is Algy who is first to reach the scene. The others are close behind him. They are helping Rupert to his feet when he realises that they aren't looking at him. They are staring at something behind him. He swings round to see what and his own eyes pop at the sight that greets them. The top has come off the box and sticking up is the head of the wings' owner. It looks something like a bird's head, but it has a sort of horn sticking out behind on which is balanced a bit of egg-shell. The Professor is the first to speak: "I do declare, it's a pterodactyl! A real life pterodactyl!" The others stare at it in silence. Then Rupert whispers, "It's a terry-what?"

RUPERT PICKS A NAME

The creature is the strangest thing
With sort of fingers on each wing.

"Let's call it Terry, if we may.
Its proper name is hard to say."

"Terry? Why, yes! I think that's neat.
Let's take him home. He'll want to eat."

"I say!" laughs Algy. "Look at that!
He's hanging there just like a bat!"

"It is a pterodactyl," repeats the Professor and spells out the word. "You say it 'terrodaktil'," he adds. "But let's get the poor little thing out of there." And he and his servant set about gently releasing the creature from the box. It seems very friendly. "What is a . . . what you called it?" Rupert asks. "Well," says the Professor, "pterodactyls are flying creatures which vanished from the earth thousands of years ago – or so we thought." "Since its name's so hard to say," Rupert suggests, "why don't we call it simply Terry?" "H'm, Terry the pterodactyl," muses the Professor. "Yes, that's neat. Terry it shall be. Now let's get him home and find him something to eat." He picks up a fallen branch and, with his servant, holds it out to Terry who seems to know what's wanted for he hops onto it and hangs upside down. "Just like a bat!" laughs Algy. Then off they all set for the Professor's tower.

RUPERT MEETS A SARDINE LOVER

"Find out if we've got what we need
To make up pterodactyl-feed."

The old man is explaining when
His servant hurries in again.

"I let the little creature taste
All sorts of things. But what a waste!"

"He tried spaghetti, crisps and beans
But all he likes are tinned sardines."

Indoors Terry is taken off in search of whatever food pterodactyls may eat. "What an adventure!" the Professor chuckles when he and the others are settled in his study. "All because of my old junk. I made the wheels for a flying trolley. But they didn't work well. The egg came from an explorer friend who found it somewhere. Who'd have thought it would hatch? My servant must have thrown the box out thinking it was empty." And just then the servant returns.

"I've found what Terry likes," he announces. Seemingly he tried all sorts of food on the little creature without success – until he tried sardines. "He's eaten six lots," the servant says. "I'd a job to stop him eating the tins!" The Professor smiles. "We shall have to find a place suitable for pterodactyls," he says. "But until we do – and that could take time – Terry can stay here. At least we know what to feed him on!" The End.

Rupert's Paper Mouse

This little mouse was created by a well-known paper-folder, Paul Jackson of the British Origami Society. You will need a piece of paper about eight inches square. Make all folds firmly and neatly. Note: The diagrams are not all to the same scale.

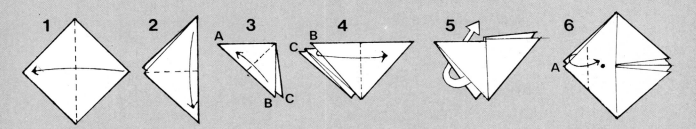

(1) Fold paper in half. (2) Repeat as shown. (3) Fold up B and C either side of A to make (4). Then fold back B as shown. Turn model over and repeat with C to get (5). Now open the model up to make (6) then fold back point A to the dot and get (7).

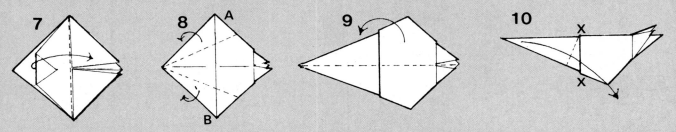

Bring back that newly-folded-back edge for (8). Fold back the new A and B along dotted lines to meet behind for (9). Double model over to get (10). (XX marks the thick fold you tuck the tail into later.) Fold tail forward along dotted line and get (11).

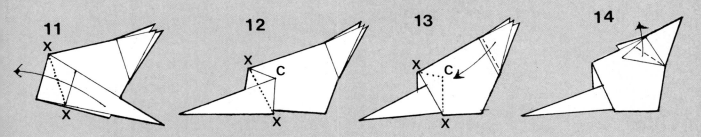

Fold it once more along the solid line for (12). Tuck C under XX as in (13). Fold back ears as shown here, then take their points up as in (14). Curl the tail and there's your mouse! You can draw an eye either side.

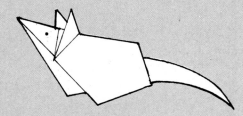

RUPERT and

*Rupert has been away to stay
With uncle for a holiday.*

"Good old Nutwood!" Rupert has been on a visit to his Uncle Bruno and it certainly has been fun. But now as familiar houses and fields slip past and the train pulls into Nutwood station, Rupert thinks, "It's good to be home!" The train stops and he gets out. The guard waves his flag and off goes the train, leaving Rupert alone. Quite alone. "Odd," he thinks. "Mummy and Daddy knew I'd be on this train."

the Sleeping Village

But no one's there to meet him when
He reaches Nutwood once again.

There's not a soul about at all,
Not even in the booking-hall.

Rupert stays put, but when after a while no one has appeared he makes for the booking-hall. Maybe Mummy and Daddy are there. But the booking-hall is as deserted as the platform. Not even the ticket-collector. Rupert begins to feel uneasy, as you do when something you know well acts in an unexpected way. He risks a peek into the booking-office. Yes! The ticket-collector and booking-clerk are there. But fast asleep!

What's going on? He takes a peep.
The staff in there are fast asleep!

41

He tries to waken them in vain.
Something's far wrong. That's very plain.

A cart stands in the station yard,
Both horse and driver snoring hard.

"There's Gaffer Jarge. He's sleeping too!
What's going on? What shall I do?"

"I'll ask the police. For goodness sake!
Not even Growler is awake!"

Rupert tries to attract the attention of the sleepers in the booking-office. But they go on sleeping with happy smiles on their faces. So he leaves his ticket, picks up his case and goes outside. The village carrier's horse and cart are there as usual and Rupert is about to say "Hello" to the old horse when he sees that *it* is fast asleep. A snore makes him look up. So is the carrier, happily asleep. "What on earth is going on?" Rupert wonders uneasily.

Something is far from right! No one to meet him. Everyone he's seen fast asleep. And, oh, so quiet! Rupert starts for home at a trot. The next person he sees is Nutwood's oldest villager, Gaffer Jarge. It's not unusual to find him dozing in the sun and usually he wakens when he is spoken to. But not today. "The police," thinks Rupert. "I'll try Constable Growler. He'll be able to tell me what's happening." And so he might – if he were awake. But he's not!

RUPERT IS TOLD THE REASON

He rushes home. He hardly dare
Think what he may find waiting there.

And yes! Exactly as he feared,
They're both asleep. My, this is weird!

"The music did it, that I know."
Rupert spins round to find a crow.

All Nutwood's in the land of dreams
Because some strange harp sang, it seems.

Rupert is really worried now. He leaves his case in the police station and sets off at a run for his own cottage. The sound of his footsteps is the loudest thing he hears. He hardly dares to think what he will find at home. He dashes up the garden path and throws open the front door. And it's as he feared. Mr. and Mrs. Bear are in their chairs, smilingly asleep. "Mummy! Daddy!" Rupert cries. "What's going on?" From behind Rupert a voice croaks, "The music did it!"

Rupert spins round to see a big crow sitting on the windowsill. "Didn't mean to scare you," the crow apologises. "But you did ask." "You said the music did it," quavers Rupert. "What music?" He approaches the crow which seems to be a friendly creature. "It was the harp," it says. "The harp the boy has." Rupert is bewildered. "What boy? What harp?" he cries. "Best you see for yourself," the crow croaks. "They're near here. Come on and I'll show you."

RUPERT HEARS THE HARP'S TALE

*The crow says, "Let me show you where
To find that strange harp, little bear."*

*"You look a kind young bear to me,"
The harp says. "Oh, please set me free!"*

*"To stop this Jack who stole me I
Performed the giant's lullaby."*

*"That may have been your only chance,
But now all Nutwood's in a trance!"*

Rupert hesitates, unwilling to leave his parents. But they show no sign of stirring and the crow keeps saying, "Come on!" So Rupert goes out and follows it. "Not far," it croaks as it leads the way up to the common. "Under the big tree there." When Rupert reaches it he gasps. Asleep against the trunk is a boy in old-fashioned clothes and he is clutching a harp. "That's it," the bird says. "The harp that put Nutwood to sleep." But Rupert is even more startled when the harp speaks: "You look a kind little bear. Please free me from this awful Jack. He stole me from my master, the gentlest of all giants. He broke into his castle and stole me as my master slept." "I *am* sorry!" Rupert says. "But my friend the crow says you put all Nutwood to sleep with your music." "I didn't mean to," the harp replies. "I thought I might stop Jack by singing my giant's lullaby. It puts ordinary folk into a deep sleep, you see. A very deep sleep."

RUPERT WAKES WITH AN IDEA

*The harp admits it can't think how
To waken Nutwood's people now.*

*So Rupert settle down and thinks,
But soon into a doze he sinks.*

*The harp takes care to make no sound
While Rupert sleeps fast on the ground.*

*"The bird's dawn chorus made me wake.
I see the course that I must take!"*

"That's all very well," Rupert tells the harp. "But it's because of you that everyone is fast asleep and won't waken." Then he remembers the crow and adds, "Except the birds." "That'll be because they sing so much themselves," the harp suggests. "Now, please, free me." But Rupert makes himself look stern and says, "Only if you waken Nutwood." "I don't know how," the harp sighs. "Then *I* must think of something," groans Rupert. "But what?" He sits down. It is getting late. He is tired. He dozes off and as darkness falls he lies down and sleeps fast, along with all Nutwood. Only the harp is awake and it is careful to make no musical sound for fear of putting Rupert into the same very deep sleep as everyone else.

With the first light the air is filled with the birds' dawn chorus. Rupert wakens and as he lies listening to the birds he has an idea. He springs up with a big smile.

RUPERT KNOWS WHAT HE NEEDS

*"I'm off to find a way to make
That chorus louder at daybreak."*

*"The answer," Rupert tells the crow,
"Is in that tower down below."*

*The door is open. Rupert knows
He's always welcome. In he goes.*

*"Were he awake I'm sure he'd lend
This stuff here to a young bear friend."*

"Thank goodness you're awake," the harp says. "Yes, and I've got an idea of how to waken the rest of Nutwood!" Rupert cries. "The birds! It was their dawn chorus that wakened me. If we can get that chorus loud enough we might waken all the village . . . and I think I know how." Then he sets off at a run. The crow catches up with him in sight of the tower home of Rupert's clever friend, the Professor. Rupert points to the tower. "I think the answer is down there!" he declares. "The

Professor's home?" the crow croaks. "Why there?" "You'll see," Rupert tells it as he lets himself into the tower. He knows his old friend would be only too glad to help if he were awake. Of course, he isn't awake, nor is his little servant when Rupert finds them in their workshop. And it's there, in an open cupboard, he sees what he wants. "I'm positive he won't mind me borrowing it in a good cause," Rupert tells the crow.

RUPERT FINDS THE STUFF

"It may look old," he tells the bird,
"But it will work well, take my word."

"In fact," says Rupert, "truth to tell,
The whole thing really works too well."

"He tried it out on our Sports Day.
The noise drove everyone away!"

He leaves a note to say what he
Has done, and signs it "Rupert B.".

The crow stares at the contents of the cupboard. They are enough to stump anyone. There's the horn of an ancient gramophone, what looks like an old radio, and an older microphone, all jumbled up with lengths of cable. "That's what we're going to waken Nutwood with," Rupert says. "I'll get something to carry it in." And off he goes to return with a trolley he has found. As he loads the equipment into it, the crow asks, "But what was all that stuff used for before." Rupert tells it: "The Professor invented it for making announcements at Nutwood Sports Day. But it turned out to be so loud the noise drove everyone away and it couldn't be used. But the Professor kept it because, he said, it might come in useful. And I think it's going to." From the Professor's desk he takes a sheet of paper and a pen and writes: "I have borrowed the loudspeaker stuff in a good cause. Will explain later. Signed Rupert B.".

RUPERT SETS IT UP

The last bits are piled in the cart,
And back towards the harp they start.

Rupert assures the harp that he
Will very shortly set it free.

"The further up the tree this goes,
The more will hear it, I suppose."

"What we need is a real, loud blast.
And this should do," he thinks at last.

With the heavily-laden trolley Rupert sets off back to the harp. "Do you know how to make that stuff work?" asks the friendly crow. "Yes, it's quite simple," Rupert says. "I helped to put it together at the Sports Day."

When they reach the big tree again Jack is still fast asleep clutching the harp. Rupert unloads the trolley, sorts out the coils of wire and fixes them to the various bits. "Aren't you going to set me free?" asks the harp. "When I've done with this,"

Rupert says, connecting up the loudspeaker – the old gramophone horn – then switching on the thing like an old radio. At once it starts to hum. "Good, still working." Rupert murmurs. "Now, the higher up I can put the loudspeaker the more people will hear it, I suppose," he adds and scrambles up the tree with it. The Professor has made it to clamp to a high post, and Rupert looks for a branch of the right thickness. High in the tree he finds one.

RUPERT ASKS THE CROW TO HELP

He tunes the set to make it play
The very loudest that it may.

He tells the friendly crow, "Now you
Have the important part to do!"

The crow says, "Right! I know my task.
The birds will all do what I ask."

And now, as Rupert sets it free,
He tells the harp, "Leave Jack to me!"

"What are you doing?" the harp asks when Rupert returns from fixing the loudspeaker. "As I told you," Rupert replies, "I was wakened by the dawn chorus this morning and I thought that, since it is this that wakens Nutwood each day, it might work now if we got it terribly loud. This stuff I'm fixing up *will* get it loud." The crow which has heard this, cries, "But the dawn chorus is over for the day!" Rupert grins. "That's where you come in. Here's what I want you to do."

The crow chuckles as it listens to Rupert's instructions. "Shouldn't be too difficult," it croaks when he is done. "I get on well with most of the Nutwood birds . . . and I'm sure I can change the minds of any who might be unwilling!" "Then off you go!" cries Rupert and away flies the crow. "I say!" It's the harp talking. "If your plan works then Jack will wake up too." As he prises Jack's grip off the harp, Rupert says, "Yes, I shall have to see to that, shan't I?"

RUPERT MEETS THE BIRD CHORUS

Around Jack's legs his scarf he twists,
And straps a belt about his wrists.

A flock of birds swarms into sight.
The crow has done his job, all right!

"No trouble!" says the friendly crow.
"Splendid!" cries Rupert. "Off we go!"

"Now, birds, imagine that it's dawn.
I'm going to switch the speaker on."

It's as well Jack's fast asleep, for Rupert has to move him about quite a bit to get the belt from round his waist. With it he binds the boy's wrists together. Then he uses his own scarf to tie Jack's ankles securely. He inspects his handiwork then tells the harp, "There! Now Jack can wake up any time he likes and he won't be able to touch you." Just then there comes the fruff-fruff of hundreds of wings and into sight flies a flock of birds of all sorts.

Rupert has seldom seen so many birds in one place. They seem to be everywhere. "As I said, it was no trouble," the friendly crow tells Rupert. "Glad to come, they were. Said today's dawn chorus was a fat lot of good with nobody wakening. Happy to try again." "Right," Rupert says. "Get them ready, please." The crow croaks an order and the birds rise in a flock. "I'm going to switch on the loudspeaker," Rupert calls. "Imagine it's dawn. Get ready!"

RUPERT WAKENS NUTWOOD

"Just sing as loudly as you like.
But try to sing into the mike."

They warble, each and every bird,
A sound like no one's ever heard!

It's worked! And all of Nutwood now
Comes streaming up to stop the row.

They can't believe that Rupert's right!
They've been asleep a day and night?

"Now, when I shout 'Go!' sing as loudly as you can!" Rupert tells the birds. "And try to sing towards the microphone, please!" "We're ready!" caws the crow. "Then . . .GO!" Rupert cries. The twittering, cawing, cooing and singing is almost deafening. And that's *before* Rupert turns up the volume. When he does, the air seems to shake with the noise. Rupert covers his ears and Jack starts awake, eyes popping, as the loudest dawn chorus ever breaks over Nutwood.

"If Jack's awake my plan's working," Rupert realises. And sure enough, in no time a string of Nutwooders led by Mr. Bear and PC Growler are streaming up to complain about the noise. Rupert switches off and signals to the birds to stop. "What's all this?" demands Growler sternly. "Yes, what are you playing at?" adds Mr. Bear. "It's the only way I could waken you!" protests Rupert. "Waken?" repeat the assembled Nutwooders. "But we haven't been asleep!"

RUPERT TELLS WHAT HAPPENED

"Who is this boy? And whose this harp?"
Snaps Growler. "Tell me, and be sharp!"

Jack tells his tale, the harp does too,
And everyone cries, "So, it's true!"

The harp asks, "Take me where I'll sing
A song which shall my master bring."

"You stole the harp, Jack, so it's fair,"
Says Growler, "that you take it there."

"It's true! All Nutwood's been asleep for a whole day and a night!" Everyone turns to see who is supporting Rupert. It's the crow. Now no one seems to know what to say. Then PC Growler splutters, "I – I don't understand this. Who's this boy? Why's he tied up? What's this harp doing here? Tell me and sharp!" So with the help of the crow, the harp and even Jack, Rupert tells the story. Everyone exclaims. Growler unties Jack and glares at him. Jack cringes.

Tutting and twittering about how behindhand they must be, the Nutwooders scurry back to the village. Only Rupert, Mr. Bear, Growler, the harp and Jack are left. "Now how do we get the harp back to the giant?" Rupert wonders. The harp speaks up. "There is a cairn some way from here where, if I sing, my master will hear and collect me. It *is* some way, though." "Then as Jack stole you," Growler says, "it's only fair that he should carry you there!"

RUPERT SHOWS THE WAY

So Jack sets off with heavy heart,
Both harp and Rupert in the cart.

At last, upon a clifftop high,
The place the harp wants, they espy.

"What? Wait to see my master? No!"
The harp says. "Please, you must all go!"

So homeward now they wend their way.
They hear the harp begin to play.

It now turns out that the harp doesn't know how to get to the cairn from here. But it so happens that Rupert knows the cairn. "A heap of big stones on a cliff," he says. "I know how to get there. I don't mind showing the way." "Good of you," Growler says. "But no reason for you to walk!" So Rupert and the harp are put in the trolley and Jack is told to start pulling – and hard! By the time the cairn comes into sight he's feeling very sorry for himself.

At the cairn the harp is unloaded and, as it asks, wedged on top of it. "My master will hear me from here," it says. "Oh, may we stay to see him?" Rupert pleads. "Oh, no!" cries the harp. "That would not be a good idea! Please, go." And so the others set off for Nutwood. As they go, Growler tells Jack, "It wouldn't have been a good idea for you to have been there when the giant comes – no matter how gentle he is."

In the distance the harp begins to sing.

Rupert is wakened by a sound
Of someone outside prowling round.

By moonlight, just as bright as day,
He sees a giant steal away.

"Last night someone – I can't think who –
Seems to have left this thing for you."

A souvenir, for him to keep,
Of how he found Nutwood asleep!

In bed Rupert smiles as he recalls Growler packing Jack off to his own village after a lecture about this not being "a fairy tale land where you steal harps just because they're owned by giants". Then he falls asleep, but only to be wakened in the middle of the night by a sound from outside. Sleepily he rises and looks out. A very large figure is tiptoeing away in the moonlight. He blinks a long blink and the figure is gone. Did he imagine it?

In the morning he is even less sure whether he saw or imagined the large figure in the garden. But at breakfast he finds out. Mr. Bear greets him with, "Look! A present for you. Someone – I can't think who – left it on the doorstep last night." It is a harp, a tiny gold one, exactly like the one that sang Nutwood to sleep. A note with it says simply, "Thank you!" "It's lovely!" cries Rupert. "I shall keep it always to remind me of my sleeping village!" The End.

Your Own Rupert Story

*Title:*_____

Why not try colouring the pictures below and writing a story to fit them?
Write your story in four parts, one for each picture, saying what it shows.
Then, faintly in pencil, print each part neatly on the lines under its
picture. When they fit, go over the printing with a ball-pen. There is
space at the top for a title.

_____

_____

_____

_____

_____

_____

RUPERT

*Says Dr. Lion, "Why I'm here,
Is Beppo's owner's ill, I fear."*

Beppo the pet monkey has always been one of Rupert's favourites, even though he is a little scamp. So Rupert is concerned when one morning he sees Dr. Lion going into Beppo's home. "Beppo's owner is not well," he tells Rupert as he hurries indoors. "Poor old lady," thinks Rupert. "Perhaps I can help by looking after Beppo for her, at least for the day. I know, I'll go and ask if I may."

Beppo and the Kite

*"Beppo's poor mistress ill? Then he
Might be much better off with me."*

*"D'you think," asks Rupert, "that I may
Look after Beppo for the day?"*

"That's kind of you," says the little maid who answers the door when Rupert makes his offer. "Wait here and I'll ask." When she returns she has Beppo with her. "We're very grateful," she tells Rupert. "The doctor says peace and quiet are what's needed – and that's not easy with Beppo about the place." Certainly Beppo seems happy about the arrangement and soon Rupert and he are heading for Rupert's cottage.

*His owner's just too glad to let
The young bear take care of her pet.*

Says Mr. Anteater, "How kind,
That you this little one should mind."

"The little one", though, decides that
He wants to have the old one's hat.

He crams it on his head and flees.
Cries Rupert, "Do come back here, please!"

Beneath the hat he can't see, which
Means he sprawls headlong in a ditch.

Mr. Anteater is nice but just a bit pompous, and, of course, it has to be him the pair meet on their way. "How very kind of you," the old fellow says when Rupert explains why Beppo is with him. At first, Beppo is a bit wary of this strange creature, but he soon gets over that when his attention is caught by the other's top hat, tall and shiny. And, being Beppo, needless to say, he makes a dive for it the moment Mr. Anteater turns his back to go.

Rupert is horrified. "No, Beppo!" he shouts. But the monkey crams the top hat on his own head, as he's seen Mr. Anteater wear it, and bolts. Rupert races after him. But, fast as he runs, Beppo is faster, even burdened with his oversize hat. The chase ends only when Beppo, who, of course, can't see where he is going, sprawls headlong into a ditch – a very wet and not very clean ditch. "Oh, no!" cries Rupert as the top hat bobs in the water.

*Rupert returns the hat and tries
For Beppo to apologise.*

*So they go home where Mrs. Bear
Says, "Not that Beppo! Do take care!"*

*"His fall into the ditch has made
Poor Beppo soggy, I'm afraid."*

*Cries Mrs. Bear, "Just as I thought, he
Simply can't stop being naughty."*

Rupert rescues the hat and, after shaking the worst of the ditch-water from it, takes it and Beppo back to Mr. Anteater. At first Mr. Anteater stares, quite speechless, at them as poor Rupert desperately tries to apologise. But he's a good sort at heart, and soon he sees the funny side. "At least the water didn't get inside it," he says. And so off go Rupert and Beppo again. But when they reach Rupert's house his Mummy who knows Beppo of old, is not altogether welcoming. "Not that mischief, Beppo!" she exclaims. "Well, just be sure you keep him under control." And when Rupert explains why Beppo is soaked and has to be stripped and dried, Mrs. Bear looks more doubtful still about their guest. And, of course, the moment he is dry and warm again, Beppo, just has to show how right she is by shinning up the curtains she is hanging. "The little wretch!" she cries. "As I thought, he just can't help being naughty!"

RUPERT MAKES A SWING

It's best you shouldn't see her frown
When Beppo pulls her curtains down.

"That does it then!" cries Mrs. Bear.
"Just get that mischief out of there."

Thinks Rupert, "Now, I'm sure I could
Do something with that rope and wood."

Soon Beppo, lucky little thing,
Has got himself a splendid swing.

To make things worse, Mrs. Bear's angry shout startles Beppo who tries to scramble down her nice clean curtains and drags them with him so that they end up a tangled heap on the floor. "That does it!" storms Mrs. Bear. And Rupert has seldom seen her look so cross. "Just get that little mischief out of here!" "But I've said I'd look after him all day!" Rupert protests. "Then he must stay in the box-room," Mrs. Bear decides. "And behave himself!"

The box-room is a dull place where all kinds of tools and bits and pieces are stored. Not the sort of place in which to spend the day. So as Beppo struggles back into his clothes, Rupert looks around for something to entertain him. And he spies something. There is lots of wood, screws, rope and a pair of steps. Rupert sets to work and in no time has rigged up a swing. "There, that should keep you amused," he says as Beppo happily leaps onto it.

RUPERT TRIES OUT HIS KITE

"It's really such a lovely day,"
Says Podgy. "Do come out and play."

"It's nice and breezy so let's try
And see how well your kite can fly."

It's likely, Rupert says, they might
Find some adventure with the kite.

Podgy can't stop it when the breeze
Carries the kite towards some trees.

Rupert feels at a loss without Beppo and wanders into the garden just as Podgy Pig appears at the gate. "It's a lovely day," he says. "Do come out and play." "Right," Rupert agrees. "But let's have a look in my toy cupboard and see if we can get any ideas for a game." And it's there that Podgy spots Rupert's kite. "Oh, come on, do let's fly it!" he urges. "It's nice and breezy. Let's see how well it goes!" So Rupert lifts out the kite, but he says, "You know, I always think there's something strange about this kite." And later while Podgy is tying what they call "chickens" on the kite's tail, Rupert explains, "I've never taken this kite out without its leading me into an adventure." But all Podgy says is, "Well, that sounds fine. May I fly it first and see?" And he does – see, that is. For no sooner have they launched the kite than the wind quite suddenly strengthens a lot and drags Podgy towards some trees.

61

RUPERT GOES AFTER THE KITE

The kite gets tangled in the leaves.
In vain poor Podgy tugs and heaves.

Says Rupert, "I'll climb up the tree,
Or else we'll never get it free."

"Oh, do look out, for goodness sake!
I think the tree is going to break!"

To save it Rupert has to jump,
And comes down with a nasty bump.

The kite drags Podgy along at such a rate that, plump as he is, he leaves Rupert who is a good runner, well behind. When Rupert does catch up it is only because Podgy has had to stop. The kite has got tangled in a tree and he is trying to free it by tugging at the string. "That's no use," Rupert pants. "You'll make it worse. Someone must climb up and free it." He studies the tree which is young and slender. "I better go," he says. "I'm lighter than you."

Rupert is also a good climber which Podgy most certainly is not. So up the slim trunk he shins. But as he gets near the kite the tree bends in an alarming way. It's not going to take his weight. "Do look out for goodness sake!" yells Podgy. "It's going to break!" "I can't risk breaking it," Rupert shouts back. "It's in someone's garden. I'm going to drop!" And down he comes with a bump. But he's an agile little bear and, though he's shaken, he isn't really hurt.

RUPERT FETCHES BEPPO

"Beppo can climb. What's more he's light.
Let's send him up to get the kite."

"Hey, Beppo, I've a job for you.
Come on! I'll tell you what to do."

"Good Beppo! Up you go! That's right!
And fetch us down the lovely kite."

Beppo's still working up on high
As dear old Mrs. Sheep comes by.

"Since even you're too heavy for the tree, what do we do now?" asks Podgy. Rupert thinks hard. Then – "Got it!" he cries. "Beppo, of course! He's light and can climb well. If only we can get him to understand what's wanted. It's worth a try, anyway. I'm off home to fetch him." But when Rupert dashes into the box-room he finds that Beppo has become bored with his swing and is staring wistfully out of the window. "I've a job for you!" Rupert cries. "Come on!"

Back at the tree Beppo doesn't need any urging to go up it. But whether he understands what Rupert and Podgy want him to do is another matter. But by good luck he, in fact, does what is needed. Attracted by the kite, he begins to play with it and soon he is dangling it down to the pals by its string. Rupert and Podgy are so caught up watching Beppo that neither notices that approaching across the common, laden with her shopping, is old Mrs. Sheep.

RUPERT HELPS MRS. SHEEP

*She greets the chums but doesn't see
That naughty Beppo up the tree.*

*She bleats and all her shopping drops
When on her shoulder Beppo hops.*

*Rupert scolds Beppo, then the friends
Carry her things to make amends.*

*Invited in by her, they stare
At an old portrait hanging there.*

Rupert has just got the kite safely under his arm when Mrs. Sheep, who is a pleasant old soul, greets the pals. And, of course, she admires the kite which means that Rupert tells her the story of their chase after it and how Beppo has rescued it from the tree for them. "Well, where is the little thing, now?" asks Mrs. Sheep who hasn't seen him up the tree. She finds out at that moment. For onto her shoulder Beppo springs, attracted by the flowers in her hat! Poor Mrs. Sheep gives a great bleat and drops all her shopping. Rupert grabs the monkey from her shoulder, scolds him severely, then with Podgy sets about picking up the shopping. "Do let us carry it home for you," Rupert offers. "It's the least we can do to apologise for Beppo." And that's how the pals wind up at Mrs. Sheep's cottage where they are invited indoors. There, their attention is caught by a portrait of an important-looking sheep in robes.

64

RUPERT LEARNS OF A MYSTERY

"That is my uncle, once the Mayor.
He hid a fortune here somewhere."

Then Podgy gives a warning shout.
They turn to see what it's about.

It's Beppo! And see what he's at!
Destroying Mrs. Sheep's best hat.

They yell. He knows he's in the wrong,
And from the window dives headlong.

Mrs. Sheep sees the pals studying the portrait. "That is a painting of my uncle who was once the Mayor of Nutchester. He was a very important person. He built this cottage and he hid, or so it's said, some of his fortune around here. But I have searched every corner and found no trace of it. So perhaps it's all just a tale." Before she can say anything else Podgy gives a shout and points across the room. The others swing round. Mrs. Sheep bleats and Rupert groans.

Of course, they should have known better than to turn their backs on Beppo for a moment. For there he perches on the back of a chair where Mrs. Sheep has put down the hat which so caught his eye earlier. And he is taking it to pieces, flower by flower. "Hi, stop that!" Rupert yells as everyone makes a dash for Beppo. But Beppo doesn't wait. He knows he's done wrong and he leaps for the window, dives headlong through it and scampers away.

They dash outside and look around,
But Beppo's nowhere to be found.

Says Mrs. Sheep, "Do stay to tea.
The monkey will run home, you'll see."

They've hardly finished their first cup,
When Rupert gasps, "Oh! Smoke! What's up?"

The chimney must be blocked, they fear.
"The mess!" wails Mrs. Sheep. "Oh, dear!"

Rupert and Podgy dash outside in the hope of catching Beppo but not a trace of the scamp is to be seen. "This is awful!" Rupert groans. "After all, I'm supposed to be taking care of him." Old Mrs. Sheep overhears this and calls, "Don't you worry. He'll run straight home, you'll see. And he hasn't really harmed my hat. So, both of you, do stay to tea." But as he and Podgy troop indoors Rupert is thinking, "This is a poor adventure the kite's got us into!"

Still, tea by the fire seems a good idea and the pals happily settle down to it. But not for long. They've scarcely finished the first cup before smoke billows into the room from the fireplace. "That smoke!" Rupert gasps. "The chimney must be blocked!" And Mrs. Sheep wails, "Oh, the mess! Everything will be covered in soot!" "Let's go out and have a look at the chimney," Podgy suggests. But Rupert is already on his way. He's had a thought.

*"That's Beppo up there and he's got
A slate across the chimney pot!"*

*Sighs Rupert, "Really! What a clown!
Let's take these steps and get him down."*

*"Now, off there, Beppo! Come to me,
Then we can let the smoke go free."*

*To put the slate back Rupert goes,
But something through the opening shows.*

Rupert's thought is that the cause of this latest trouble might be the same as for most of today's bother – Beppo. And he's right. For when he looks up at the chimney, there is Beppo on the chimney pot, sitting on a slate he's taken from the roof. "Right, Podgy. Let's get him down," sighs Rupert. So the pals borrow a ladder from Mrs. Sheep and as they carry it to the chimney stack Rupert says, "What a clown that Beppo is. He'd be funny if he weren't so awful."

This time Beppo doesn't seem to think that he's done anything wrong and he happily waits for Rupert as he scales the ladder. He even helps when Rupert makes it plain that he wants the slate taken off the chimney so that the smoke can escape. Then he follows Rupert along the ridge of the roof when he goes to replace the slate. It is then Rupert makes a discovery. He is just about to put back the slate when, through a small hole, he sees something.

"Yes, something's here. What can it be?
Let's have it out and then we'll see."

Then from the hole a bag he hauls.
"Is that the treasure?" Podgy calls.

It's not the treasure, but a note
That Mrs. Sheep's old uncle wrote.

"He hid his fortune amid three
Big stones. But, oh, where can they be?"

Rupert reaches into the hole the slate has so far covered and pulls out an oilskin bag that has been lodged on a rafter. "I say, Rupert, do you think that's the fortune Mrs. Sheep's uncle hid?" It's Podgy who has followed Rupert up the ladder. "It's a jolly small fortune if it is," Rupert says. "Feels to me as if there's only a piece of paper in this bag. But, look, you take it down and I'll follow with Beppo." And Rupert tosses the bag to Podgy.

On the ground the pals hold their breath as Mrs. Sheep opens the bag and produces a piece of paper. "My goodness!" she says. "It *is* about the fortune. It's in uncle's writing and it says, 'You must search amid three large stones'." The pals are jubilant. "Three large stones", well, they shouldn't be hard to find. But quite a long while afterwards they have changed their minds. Search as they may around the cottage, there is no sign of any three large stones.

"No luck so far? Well, go and play
And try again another day."

The breeze is blowing as before,
So they try out the kite once more.

As to their kite the two pals cling,
Beppo leaps up and grabs the string.

Perhaps he thinks, as well he might,
Once more he's got to fetch the kite.

The pals aren't sorry when Mrs. Sheep appears at the front door and says, "No luck, eh? Then I think you ought to stop now and go and play. You can try another day. You've tried hard." And it's true. The chums *have* tried hard. But the only big stones they've found around the cottage are the doorstep and the flagstone in front of it. No three stones. So, though disappointed, they are glad to break off.

As they make their way home the breeze springs up, so they decide to try the kite again. With this kite, though, they might have seen that something odd was bound to happen. The breeze suddenly turns to a gale. The pals cling as hard as they can to the kite's string but it is all they can do to keep their feet. Then Beppo joins in, perhaps thinking the pals want him to fetch the kite again. He leaps for the string and starts up it. By now the wind is pulling them to the wood behind Mrs. Sheep's cottage.

RUPERT FINDS THE STONES

They're dragged towards the forest trees,
And then the kite drops with the breeze.

It's caught up in a giant oak.
To get it down will be no joke!

"There's Beppo, Podgy! And just see!
The stones he's on! Why, there are three!"

The pals feel sure beyond a doubt,
These are the stones the note's about.

The kite moves so fast that Podgy has to let go and Rupert is dragged even faster after it. Then when it is well over the wood the wind drops . . . and so do the kite and Beppo. The pals plunge into the trees heading for where the kite came down. They find it caught up in a big oak. "It's going to be no joke getting this free," Rupert groans. "But first things first. We've got to find Beppo." And, indeed, of the little monkey there isn't a sign.

In fact, the kite isn't hard to free, as a sharp tug by Podgy reveals, and the pals take it with them when they search for Beppo. It is quite a while later that Rupert climbs a tree to search a clearing and spies Beppo. He is playing on a group of stones . . . three stones! Rupert yells to Podgy and they race to the stones. Yes, three of them. And big. The pals exchange looks. "Oh, Beppo!" Rupert laughs. "I think you've just led us to a fortune!"

RUPERT DIGS UP THE BOX

"The treasure, Podgy, I'll be bound,
Is buried in this bit of ground."

So back to Mrs. Sheep he flies.
"Please, have you any spades?" he cries.

With Mrs. Sheep, a trowel and spade,
He heads back to the forest glade.

"And there it is! We weren't wrong!
The fortune that's been lost so long!"

What makes the pals even more sure they have found where the fortune is buried, is the ring of small stones in the middle of the three big ones. "They were put there to mark something jolly important," says Rupert. "We've got to dig and for that we need tools. Wait here!" And with that, he dashes back to Mrs. Sheep's cottage. She is at the door as he runs up the path. "Please," he pants, "have you any spades. I think we've found your treasure!"

One spade and a trowel is all they can find, but with those – and Mrs. Sheep at his heels – Rupert hurries back to the stones. "What a tangle this wood is," gasps Mrs. Sheep. "No wonder I never found the stones!" At last, though, they reach the stones where Podgy and Beppo are waiting and at once the digging starts. Not much later Mrs. Sheep is gazing at a box the pals have uncovered. "There it is," Rupert declares. "You uncle's lost fortune!"

Says Mrs. Sheep, "I have a key.
Perhaps it fits. Let's go and see."

It does! And in the box they find
Gold, cash and jewels of every kind.

Adventure's over! When they try
To launch the kite it will not fly.

"Though Beppo's helped a lot, I know,
I shan't be sad to see him go."

Rupert heaves the heavy box from the hole and tugs at the lid. It won't budge. "We'll have to force it," he mutters. "No, wait!" says Mrs. Sheep. "There's an old key in my bureau. Let's see if that fits." So back to the cottage they troop to find the key. And, yes, it does work. The rusted hinges creak. Up comes the lid. And everyone gasps. The old box is crammed with gold, jewels and money!

Later – after Mrs. Sheep has thanked them over and over again – the pals decide to launch the kite as they walk home. It refuses to fly. "That," says Rupert, "means that this adventure is over."

When they reach Rupert's cottage Mrs. Bear is told the whole story of Mrs. Sheep's fortune and the part Beppo played in finding it. "H'm," she says with a little smile, "I suppose that makes up for his being quite so naughty. Still, I shan't be sorry to see him go home." The End.

Rupert's Decoration

Anyone can make this decoration. It's so simple that you could easily make enough to decorate a Christmas trees. Try it out with a sheet of paper about eight inches square.

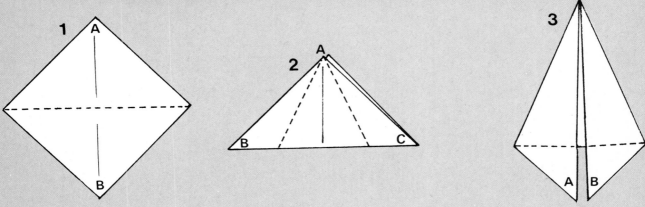

Fold the square to make a centre line AB (1), then take B up to A to give you (2). Fold edges AB and AC along the dotted lines to the centre, giving you (3). Now fold back the points A and B along the dotted lines. You have (4).

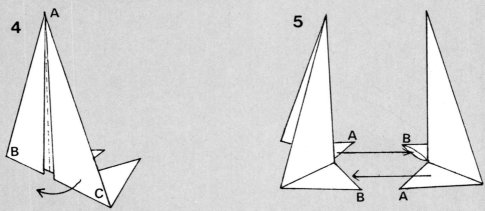

Bend the edges AB and AC towards each other so that the model looks like those in (5). Slot the points A into the pockets B to lock the two parts together.

Finally, fix a hanging thread through the points. If you can make the two parts of different coloured papers so much the better – or you could paint them. You might also try making the decoration in different sizes.

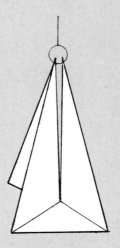

73

RUPERT

*"Sardines round here are very rare
Since Terry came," says Mrs. Bear.*

"Why don't we ever have sardines?" Rupert asks one evening. "There isn't one to be had in Nutwood since the Professor has had that Terry staying with him," says Mrs. Bear. Ah, yes! Still fresh in Rupert's mind is the adventure of the go-cart and the pterodactyl egg that hatched in mid-air. The baby pterodactyl – Terry – went to stay with the Professor and from the start showed an unending appetite for sardines.

and Terry's Return

And Rupert knows just what she means.
The little creature loves sardines.

He thinks the old Professor may
Be of some help, so calls next day.

Next day Rupert calls on the Professor to see how Terry is. He finds him with another clever friend, the Wise Old Goat. "Hello! What brings you here?" the Professor asks. So Rupert explains about the sardine shortage which made him think of Terry. "Sardines?" smiles the Wise Old Goat. "Well, there ought to be enough of them soon." He chuckles. But the Professor looks as if he thinks his friend has said too much.

The Wise Old Goat says, "Soon there'll be
Enough sardines. Just wait and see!"

John Harrold.

RUPERT HEARS A SAD STORY

*"Terry does not fit in here so
We think it best that he should go."*

*"Although he does mean well enough,
The others think he's far too rough."*

*"Because the other birds won't play
He's more unhappy every day."*

*"To send him home is only fair.
The trouble is we don't know where."*

Seemingly unaware of the Professor's look, the Wise Old Goat goes on: "Terry doesn't fit in here. He belongs to thousands of years ago. All he will eat is sardines. The other flying things – birds – are scared to play with him." Just then a flock of birds swoops overhead, pursued by Terry, vainly trying to make friends. "So," the Goat goes on, "he gets unhappier by the day and mopes around eating too many sardines. The Professor has asked my advice about getting him to his proper home . . . wherever that is." "Taking Terry home?" cries Rupert. "How? Where?" The Professor sighs: "That's the trouble, we don't know. I'm not sure where his egg was found so we can't take him back there." At that moment Terry comes down squawking. "He's bored," the Professor says. "He wants to go in." So he and the Wise Old Goat hold the Goat's staff between them, Terry climbs glumly onto it and is taken indoors.

RUPERT'S FRIEND HAS AN IDEA

All he can do is hang around
And gorge on sardines by the pound.

"Terry's an ancient creature so
It's back in time that he should go!"

"My History Clock I mean to use
To take him to what age we choose."

"Ah, clever Goat!" the old man cries.
"Let's do it now. You know, time flies!"

Indoors the Professor's servant is opening tins of sardines. At once Terry hops down and starts devouring them. "He does it because he is miserable," the Professor sighs. "We must get him home. But where?" The Wise Old Goat has been thinking. "The question isn't *where* his home is but *when*," he says. "No matter where we took him there'd be no other pterodactyls. He is from a long gone age. We must take him back in *time* . . . and I think I know how!"

"Your History Clock!" cries Rupert. The Professor looks perplexed. "Don't you know about it?" Rupert asks. "It can whisk you back and forward in time. Once I fiddled with it and was taken back centuries – but that's another story." "And it can take Terry back to his own ancient time?" cries the old man. "Where is this wonderful clock, you clever Goat?" "In my castle," the Goat says. "Then let's go there now," urges the Professor. "Come on! Time flies, eh? Ha, ha!"

77

RUPERT ENTICES TERRY

The servant's sent to get the car,
But Terry won't get on his bar.

So Rupert hints that if he's good,
He'll have more of his favourite food.

The old man says, "Now let's away
And get this done without delay!"

Terry gets in an awful pet
When he finds there's no food just yet.

The Professor has perked up now that there's a chance of solving the Terry problem and his servant is sent to fetch the car. But it isn't to be as easy as that. When the Wise Old Goat and the Professor try to coax Terry onto the staff he uses as a perch he refuses to budge. No amount of pleading will move him. In the end Rupert succeeds by filling a basket with tins of sardines and making for the car. Squawking, Terry flies after him, following him into the back seat, his eyes glued on the basket. Then the Goat takes his place, the Professor climbs behind the wheel and with a rattle and a bang off they go.

From the start Rupert has to fend off Terry who is determined to have the sardines. Gradually the little creature gets crosser as he sees that there's to be no food yet. He sets up such an awful squawking that Rupert is mightily relieved when the Goat's castle appears.

RUPERT SEES A STRANGE CLOCK

How Terry squawks and squeals! He means
To get at those cans of sardines.

He's making such an awful din,
He must be grabbed and carried in.

"It's time now to discuss our plans.
So, Rupert, open up those cans."

"Now that he's quiet, no time to lose!
Here is the time-piece we shall use."

By the time the car pulls up at the Wise Old Goat's front door Terry is quite out of hand, squawking, beating his leathery wings and making darts at the sardines in Rupert's basket. Rupert knows that Terry isn't really greedy and that he is just miserable. But, greedy or not, Terry is too much for him, and the Professor has to come to his rescue, grappling Terry out of the car, tucking him firmly under his arm and hustling him indoors.

The Wise Old Goat ushers Rupert and the Professor into his workroom. Rupert can see no sign of the History Clock which more than once has taken him through time. But before they can do anything or discuss plans Terry has to be quietened so Rupert opens the sardine tins. As soon as he is busy guzzling, the Goat crosses to a curtain and pulls it aside to reveal what looks like an old clock in a glass cabinet. "My History Clock, Professor!" he announces.

RUPERT HAS TROUBLE

The problem is to find if they
Have chosen the right time, they say.

"Someone had better go to see,"
The old man says. "It best be me."

Now Terry starts his tricks again
And Rupert chases him in vain.

Somebody must control him so
It's plain the old man cannot go.

The glass around the Clock is to prevent anyone being carried off by accident, the Goat explains. "We shall put Terry in the cabinet," he goes on, "set the Clock for the right period and switch it on from out here. We shall set it for as far back as it goes." "But what if it isn't the right time?" asks Rupert. "Then," says the Professor, "one of us will have to go first and find out, since Terry would not be able to bring himself back. It best be me. I suppose there *is* some way I can get myself back?" "Oh, yes! The Returner," says the Goat and takes from the wall a thing like an old pocket watch. Just then Terry, who has finished the sardines, becomes fretful and starts to squawk and barge about the room. Rupert tries to grab him and is sent spinning. The Goat does no better. Only the Professor is able to overpower the little scamp. At once Rupert sees that without the Professor Terry will be uncontrollable.

RUPERT VOLUNTEERS TO GO

"As you must work the Clock, it's clear,"
Says Rupert, "I should volunteer."

"Now here's a thing you must not lose.
It brings you back here when you choose."

The Clock's hands are now set to show
As far back as the thing can go.

"Remember, have a good look round
Then come and tell us what you've found."

The Wise Old Goat thinks the same. "We can't have him barging about," he says. "He may damage the Clock. Yet only you, Professor, can control him." "So it's plain *he* can't go back in time," says Rupert. "And you have to work the Clock. So it looks as if I had better volunteer." The Professor is about to argue but the Goat interrupts: "Oh, good, Rupert! With the Returner to get you back, it is quite safe." Rupert wishes he felt as sure.

The Goat hangs the Returner around Rupert's neck and tells him, "To return to the present press the button on this." Then without further ado he ushers Rupert into the cabinet and joins him just long enough to adjust the hands on the Clock. "Now when you get to where you're going," he says, "take a good look round then come back and tell us so that we can decide if it's right for Terry." He leaves the cabinet. "Ready?" he asks. Rupert gulps and nods.

Now all is set. "Good luck! Goodbye!"
Gone in the winking of an eye!

Only a drowsiness he knows
As back through countless years he goes.

"I've got here! But where can it be?
My goodness, I think I'm at sea!"

A voice asks, "Where's the other bear?
On my Ark there must be a pair."

Although he has travelled through time with the History Clock before, Rupert can't help feeling nervous. "Relax," the Wise Old Goat calls. Rupert breathes deeply. "Be careful . . ." starts the Professor. But just then the Goat pulls the switch. The Professor's voice seems to fade. Rupert is aware of his old friend staring at him. He feels, oh, so drowsy and in the instant of falling asleep has a lovely, drifting, floating-through-the-air feeling.

Rupert opens his eyes. "I've got here!" he thinks. "But where?" He rises and looks about him. "Gosh! I'm on a ship at sea!" he gasps. Next moment he almost jumps out of his skin as a hand falls on his shoulder and a voice asks, "Where's the other one?" The speaker is an old man. "Other what?" Rupert stammers. "Bear, of course!" chides the other. "You know perfectly well there's two of everything on the Ark . . . sure as my name's Noah."

RUPERT GETS A CLUE FROM NOAH

"Since this is Noah's Ark it's clear,
Do you have pterodactyls here?"

Says Noah, "Sort of dragons – no!
They must have vanished moons ago."

A bossy boy calls, "Father dear,
We don't let animals out here!"

"He's right," says Noah. "Off you go!
I'm looking for a dove, you know."

"Noah!" Rupert exclaims. "You mean *the* Noah?" "Why, is there another?" the old man asks. "Well, there's a sort of toy one who comes to Nutwood," says Rupert. Noah is bewildered. "Look, who are you?" he demands. "I'm Rupert Bear from Nutwood and I'm looking for pterodactyls," says Rupert. "Are there any aboard?" "Pterodactyls?" Noah repeats. "No, none here. Heard of them, I think. Vanished moons ago. A bit like dragons, they were. Neither birds nor beasts."

Dragons! An idea starts to form in Rupert's mind. But before he can get it clear a voice rings out: "Father, dear! You know we don't let the animals out here! This bear should be in with the others." "B-but I'm not that sort of bear!" Rupert protests. In vain. "Japheth is quite right, you know," says Noah. "Off you go and let me get on with looking for the dove I sent out." Protesting still, Rupert is hustled off by Noah's son.

83

RUPERT QUITS THE ARK

"Now back you go with all the rest,"
The boy says. "Folk like me know best."

Thinks Rupert, "I'm not staying here.
The time has come to disappear!"

"Well," Rupert says. "That wasn't long!
But I'm afraid the time was wrong."

"Still, Noah helped more than he knew.
Something he said gave me a clue."

This Japheth really is an unpleasantly bossy youth. "Now don't argue," he snaps. "Can't think what gets into you animals. Remember, folk like me know best!" And he bundles Rupert into what looks like a zoo, a jolly crowded zoo! Something bangs on Rupert's chest. Of course! The Returner. And plainly now's the time to use it. At once Rupert presses the button. He feels a buzzy sensation, then the drowsiness. The cries of amazement around him fade away . . .

"Thank goodness, you're safe!" The first voice Rupert hears when he opens his eyes again is the Professor's. He's back in the Wise Old Goat's castle. He doesn't seem to have been gone for any time at all. "Whew!" he gasps. "That wasn't long!" "Well, what did you find?" clamour his old friends excitedly. How they groan when they hear that the History Clock only goes back to Noah and the Flood. "But," Rupert grins, "Noah said something that's given me an idea!"

RUPERT EXPLAINS HIS IDEA

"The pterodactyls, Noah thought,
Were dragons of an ancient sort."

"We'll ask my pal Pong-Ping to let
Young Terry meet his dragon pet."

"It's really thanks to you we got
This clue," calls Rupert. "Thanks a lot!"

"My pal Pong-Ping, I'm sure we'll find
To be both helpful and most kind."

Rupert explains: "Noah said pterodactyls were like dragons but much older. And I wondered if they might be dragons' ancestors. Then I thought of my pal Pong-Ping. He's Chinese, so's his pet dragon. Chinese honour ancestors. So I feel that at least we should let Terry and his dragon meet." "I don't quite understand," the Professor says. "But if Pong-Ping can help let's go and see him now!" And he springs up with Terry still tucked under his arm.

"It's really thanks to you and your clock we got this clue," Rupert tells the Wise Old Goat as he and the others set off. To the Professor he says, "Terry can't go back to his own time so, if he *is* a sort of dragon the best place for him in the present is where there *are* dragons. That's Pong-Ping's part of China. And since they honour ancestors there I'm sure he'd be welcome." As the pair make their way into Pong-Ping's house Rupert says, "I know Pong-Ping will help."

RUPERT INTRODUCES TERRY

"The pterodactyl! Well, I'm blessed!"
Cries Pong-Ping, plainly most impressed.

His dragon makes the humblest bow,
The sort the Chinese call "kowtow".

It honours little Terry for
It sees him as an ancestor.

"Now, come on, Terry! Let's away!
We can't just stay out there all day!"

Pong-Ping has heard the car and is at the door to greet his visitors. "The pterodactyl! Well, I'm blessed!" he exclaims when he sees Terry. "I've heard so much about him. Oh, this is a great honour!" Rupert starts to explain his idea for solving Terry's problem. "I shall be delighted to help!" Pong-Ping cries. "But about Terry being a kind of dragon, are you sure?" And just then his pet dragon appears. It advances slowly towards Terry – and bows very low!

"There!" Rupert cries. 'I'm right!" "Oh, yes!" breathes Pong-Ping. "He must recognise Terry as an ancestor to be *so* respectful! Come inside." But the pet dragon is still bowing to Terry and plainly isn't going to move until Terry does. "Oh, come on, Terry," says the Professor. "We can't stay here all day." Terry gives a squeak which the dragon seems to understand for it lifts its head, smiles and skips into the house with Terry.

RUPERT TAKES TERRY HOME

*"In China where the dragons dwell,
Young Terry will do very well."*

*"We'll take the pair to Dragon Land.
My lift to China's close at hand."*

*The old Professor leads the way.
The pet and Terry romp and play.*

*"As soon as we've lodged Terry there
We'll be right back," says Rupert Bear.*

Pong-Ping is in no doubt that Terry will do splendidly in China and so they should get him there right away. Now, as everyone who knows Nutwood is aware, Pong-Ping has a lift that goes straight to China and that is how Rupert and he are going to take Terry. But first, since there are no sardines in Dragon Land, they try Terry with dragon food – golden pearapples. Well, they go down faster than even sardines did! And so while Pong-Ping puts his pet on its lead for the trip,

the others have a farewell glass of pearappleade. Then out to the lift they go, the Professor leading the way and saying what a pity there isn't room for him in the lift as he would very much like to see China. But he is smiling as he waves them off. "And, anyway," he says, "I better go and tell Rupert's Mummy that he's gone to China to finish a splendid job he has done and will be back soon . . . and that the sardine shortage is over!" The End.

RUPERT'S OWN COUNTRYSIDE
by Alfred Bestall, MBE

Twenty-one years ago Alfred Bestall painted this picture for the Rupert Annual.
We feel today's readers deserve to see it.

RUPERT and

They're all agog with Christmas nigh.
Bored, Podgy says he can't think why.

Rupert and his chums are in Bingo's shed happily chattering about Christmas and how near it is. Everyone is excited – well, everyone except Podgy. Lounging by the door, he jeers, "Can't see what you're excited about. The food and presents are all right, I suppose." Then he slouches off. "His trouble is he's too well off," Bill says and everyone agrees. But Rupert is worried about his plump pal.

Podgy's Christmas

"The food and presents, I suppose,
Are fine," he yawns. And off he goes.

Rupert's just reached his garden gate
When someone calls, "Hi, Rupert, wait!"

Later, Rupert is turning in at his gate when someone calls his name. It is Santa Claus's helper, the little cowboy. He looks cross. And Rupert soon finds out why. "Being in these parts, I thought I'd pick up present lists to save people posting them," he says. "First one I spoke to was Podgy Pig. Never met anyone so selfish and greedy. All he wants is to eat a lot and get expensive presents."

It's Santa's helper and he says
He knows of Podgy's selfish ways.

RUPERT FLIES TO SEE SANTA

"That Podgy needs a lesson, so
I'm off to let old Santa know."

"If you want to, then you can come
To put a word in for your chum."

"Get in," he says. "We'll soon be there.
The journey takes no time by air."

So, far above the clouds they fly,
To Santa's castle in the sky.

"I'm worried about Podgy," sighs Rupert. The cowboy snorts. "Well, *Podgy* better start worrying," he says. "I'm telling Santa it's time he was taught a lesson." "Please, no!" Rupert begs. "He's just a bit spoilt." "Sorry," says the cowboy. "It's my duty to tell Santa about such folks." Then he sees how upset this makes Rupert and adds, "Look, I *must* do my duty, but you can come with me and put in a word for Podgy. We can go now. My airplane's nearby."

And off strides the cowboy to the high common with Rupert following. By the time Rupert catches up with him he is already seated in his machine. "Get in," he says. "I'll have you back in time for supper. You should be warm enough in that warm coat and scarf." Rupert clambers aboard and in no time they are high in the blue, bound for the cloudy towers of Santa's castle. "I hope I can persuade Santa not to be cross with Podgy," thinks Rupert. "He *is* my pal."

RUPERT PLEADS FOR PODGY

As soon as Santa Claus appears,
Of Podgy's selfishness he hears.

He says, "A lesson's what he needs."
"He isn't selfish!" Rupert pleads.

But Rupert leaves without a clue
To what old Santa means to do.

"Whatever Santa has in mind,"
The cowboy calls, "he's always kind."

The airplane has hardly stopped before Santa's burly figure appears. "Rupert!" he calls in his big voice. "What are you doing here?" But the old gentleman's face loses its smile when over cups of cocoa he hears the cowboy's report on Podgy. "It sounds as if he needs a lesson about Christmas," he rumbles. Then he listens to what Rupert has to say for Podgy, how he isn't truly selfish, just a bit spoilt and unthinking.

"I'll have to think about this," is all Santa will say when Rupert is finished. "And now," he smiles, "the cowboy has promised to get you home in time for supper, so off you go."

As the airplane takes off for Nutwood Rupert doubts that he has done much good for his chum. It is dusk when they land near Rupert's cottage. "So long," says the cowboy. "Sorry I had to tell Santa about your pal. But whatever Santa does will be for the best, believe me."

RUPERT WAITS FOR SANTA

And still, as Christmas Day draws near,
All Podgy does is gloat and jeer.

"Your presents, Santa's gonna leave
On Nutwood Common, Christmas Eve."

So on that cold and sparkling night
The pals are there with Rupert's light.

"Don't open them 'til Christmas Day,"
Says Santa, then he's on his way.

The days pass and Rupert and his pals do all the things that make the time before Christmas such fun. But Podgy just moons about, jeering and gloating on the rich food and expensive presents to come. Then one evening Rupert finds the cowboy waiting with a message from Santa: "He can't come down your chimneys this year, so you and your pals are to wait for him on the common on Christmas Eve." He says no more, just turns away to his airplane.

Christmas Eve. A crisp, clear night. On the snowy common above Nutwood Rupert and his pals are grouped around a lantern waiting. At last there is a tinkling of reindeer bells and with a swoosh Santa's sledge is among them. The old man climbs from his seat and swings a heavy sack from the back of the sledge. He tips a pile of parcels from it and says, "Now, no peeking until tomorrow." Then he climbs back into his sledge and soars into the night sky.

*"Hang on!" Bill says. "I rather fear
There's something most unusual here!"*

*Each gift that Santa's left behind
Is meant for Podgy Pig, they find!*

*"Well, even if there's no big toy,
There's still a lot I can enjoy!"*

*"This turned up late," says Mr. Bear.
"And just look at that spelling there!"*

Rupert and the others turn to the parcels. "I say, hang on!" says Bill. "There aren't enough to go round. We're one short!" The others check. Bill's right! "Whose can it be?" they cry. But Rupert thinks he knows. So this is the lesson Podgy is to be taught. But he's wrong. For *all* the parcels are labelled "To Podgy"! There is a shocked silence. Then the others move slowly away, leaving Podgy alone with all his presents and speechless with surprise.

Rupert wakens on Christmas morning feeling something is amiss. Of course! No big present. "Oh, well," he thinks. "There are lots of other things to enjoy." But a surprise awaits him downstairs. Under the Christmas tree is a large parcel – the shape of the model aircraft he has been hoping for. The label says "Hapy Christmas". "Santa must have been in an awful rush," laughs Mr. Bear. "He had to leave that on the doorstep. And just see how 'Happy' is spelt!"

RUPERT CALLS ON PODGY

*Then two of Rupert's pals bring round
The presents that they, too, have found.*

*Beneath a misspelt label they
Learn who has made their Christmas Day.*

*Podgy's poor Mummy can't make out
What all the visiting's about.*

*Podgy who got no gifts, she says,
Is brighter than he's been for days!*

Before Rupert can unwrap his present there is a knock at the door. Bill and Algy are there, each clutching a large present. "You too!" gasps Rupert. "They were on our doorsteps," Algy says. "All the others who got nothing last night found presents on their doorsteps too." Then Rupert notices something. The labels on the others' presents – "Hapy Christmas" again! He peels one of the labels off carefully. There is another underneath. "To Podgy" it says!

Of course, the three pals decide they must call on Podgy. But at Podgy's house they find a crowd of others with the same idea. Podgy's Mummy can't understand what's going on. "I have never known the like!" she cries. "Podgy's had nothing from Santa but he's happier than he has been in ages." Just then Podgy appears. "Happy Christmas!" he laughs. "Don't you mean 'Happy Christmas'?" Rupert asks. "What?" Podgy begins. Then he grins. "Oh dear! My awful spelling!"

RUPERT HAS A HAPPY CHRISTMAS

It seems the presents were no fun
When Podgy knew his friends' had none

They rush out at a tinkling sound.
A present's floating to the ground.

"Look! Santa writes he's glad to see
Rupert's been proved right over me!"

Now everyone is happy there,
And largely thanks to Rupert Bear!

So Podgy confesses. "When I saw you without presents I didn't want mine. I felt even more miserable. But the moment I decided you should have them I felt great and still do." "It's a shame, though, that you've got nothing from Santa," Bill says. And just then comes the sound of bells over Podgy's roof. The pals rush out to see Santa's sledge racing away and a parcel floating down attached to a parachute on which is written "To Podgy".

There is a note with the parcel. "Listen to this!" Podgy says. "It's from Santa. He writes 'Dear Podgy, Rupert told me you were not really selfish. So I gave you all the presents to see what you would do and I'm very glad to see that Rupert is right. You will like what's in this parcel, but you've already had the best present – the happiness that comes from giving instead of getting. Now you can have a truly Happy Christmas – thanks to Rupert'." The End.

Rupert's Memory Test

How good is your memory? How carefully have you read all Rupert's adventures in the annual? Find out now by studying the pictures below. Each is part of a bigger picture you will have seen in a story. When you have had a good look at them, try to answer the questions at the bottom of the page. Then check the stories to discover if you were right.

CAN YOU REMEMBER . . .

1. Who wrote what Podgy is reading?
2. What is the Professor shouting?
3. Who is the harp's true owner?
4. Rupert is travelling through what?
5. What did he hide and where?
6. Why does Rupert need these?
7. Where is Rupert going and why?
8. Who is he and where is he going?
9. Whose hat is this?
10. "Why don't we ever have . . ." What?
11. To what is the dragon bowing?
12. Whose home is this?
13. What can Rupert see?
14. Who invented this and why?
15. Who lives here?
16. Rupert is thinking about what?